MISSOURI OZARKS
LEGENDS & LORE

MISSOURI OZARKS
LEGENDS
& LORE

Cynthia McRoy Carroll

Published by The History Press
Charleston, SC
www.historypress.com

Copyright © 2021 by Cynthia McRoy Carroll
All rights reserved

Cover images: Ozark landscape. *Courtesy of goodfreephotos*; vintage linen postcard, circa 1930–45, of iconic Route 66, showing sedimentary limestone that formed when the area was an inland sea. Hooker's Cut is located between Waynesville and Rolla, Missouri. *Author's collection.*

First published 2021

Manufactured in the United States

ISBN 9781467150408

Library of Congress Control Number: 2021941090

Notice: The information in this book is true and complete to the best of our knowledge. It is offered without guarantee on the part of the author or The History Press. The author and The History Press disclaim all liability in connection with the use of this book.

All rights reserved. No part of this book may be reproduced or transmitted in any form whatsoever without prior written permission from the publisher except in the case of brief quotations embodied in critical articles and reviews.

With spending much of 2020 and some of 2021 researching and writing Missouri Ozarks Legends and Lore *while in quarantine, it seems fitting to dedicate this book to those who have crossed paths with the COVID-19 pandemic. I am mindful that just about one hundred years ago, the Spanish flu pandemic caused global devastation as well. My maternal great-grandmother Bell Francis Irwin and her infant daughter were lost to that 1918 pandemic as it moved through the Arkansas and Missouri Ozarks.*

The 1918 Spanish flu pandemic, caused by the H1N1 Influenza A virus, lasted from February 1918 to April 1920. It infected 500 million people in four successive waves, about one-third of the world's population at that time, and claimed 50 million lives globally. Although horribly tragic, this history offers hope in what we face today. Why? The flu pandemic of 1918 eventually ran its course, even without a vaccine.

CONTENTS

Acknowledgements 9
Introduction 11
1. Missouri: The Cave State 13
2. Ozark Salem Plateau Caves 23
3. Ozark Springfield Plateau Caves 31
4. Missouri Ozarks Trails 38
5. Ozark Folklore 47
6. Ozark Ghost Stories 54
7. Ozark Monster Folklore 59
8. Haunts and Curiosities of the Salem Plateau 64
9. Haunts and Curiosities of the Springfield Plateau 77
10. Ozark Witchcraft 92
11. Iron County 96
12. Madison County 104
13. New Madrid through Reynolds County 108
14. St. Francois through Warren County 117
15. St. Louis City 130
16. The Missouri Daltons 144
Bibliography 155
About the Author 159

ACKNOWLEDGEMENTS

Road-tripping during the COVID-19 pandemic to photo-document the Missouri Ozarks was not a viable option in 2020; however, the following generous people and organizations provided images for *Missouri Ozarks Legends and Lore*. I'm forever grateful to…

The Cave Winery and Distillery of Ste. Genevieve, Missouri—Laura Oliver, cave images.

The Dalton Museum of Coffeyville, Kansas—Bret Craven, interview.

Extra Innings Photography—Ruth Ann Hentschke, Katy Trail images.

The Mine at Bonne Terre—Douglas Goergens, scuba diver images.

Morse Mill Hotel—Angelia Wiley, images.

Paranormal Task Force—Tom Halstead, photographer, and Greg Meyers, president, image of moving orb.

Ste. Genevieve Tourism—Toby Carrig, director, Colonial Creole architecture media images.

Smallin Civil War Cave, media cave images.

Mark Twain Cave Complex—Tessa Hosmer, media images of Clemens's cave signature.

Mark Twain boyhood home—Megan Rapp, media images of boyhood home.

INTRODUCTION

Inspiration for writing *Missouri Ozarks Legends and Lore* is rooted in a passion for my scenic home state of Missouri and its Ozark mystique.

A road trip through the Ozarks with my Irish twin during the peak of the fall colors was the catalyst that led me to put pen to paper and create this book. As weekend road-tripping played out, the trek between Houston, Texas and St. Louis, Missouri inspired good-natured sibling rivalry and generated double dog dares that landed us in the most haunted hotel in the country: the 1896 Crescent Hotel in Eureka Springs—on Halloween, no less.

Our scenic fall foliage drive spontaneously morphed into an Ozark haunted road trip, and it was the most fun imaginable without being called out by a ghost tour guide to demonstrate an energy field. Oh wait, that really did happen! Mark Twain summed it up in 1879 when he said, "Twins amount to a permanent riot."

Note: Check out the 2001 Ken Burns documentary titled *Mark Twain* for insight into this complicated and beloved Missouri-born and raised humorist.

Chapter 1

MISSOURI

THE CAVE STATE

The Missouri Ozarks borders, generally speaking, are the Mississippi River to the east, the Missouri River to the north and state lines west and south. The Salem Plateau and Springfield Plateau comprise the Interior Highland, or Ozarks. Salem Plateau, occupying the southeast section of the state, is much larger than the Springfield Plateau, occupying the far southwest section.

The Missouri Ozarks is an enchanting, yet unsung, destination. Come along with me for an Ozark adventure into the Cave State, with its majority of more than 7,300 caves located in Ozark counties. We'll delve into folklore and legendary Missouri monsters, Dalton outlaws, paranormal nuance, geology and Ozark history and historic architecture along the way.

The memory of a cave I used to know was always in my mind, with its lofty passages, its silence and solitude, its shrouding gloom, its sepulchral echoes, its fleeting lights, and more than all, its sudden revelations.

—*Mark Twain, Missouri native*

Mark Twain, or Samuel Clemens, spent his boyhood among Missouri hills, rivers and caves. Those experiences, in tandem with the humorist's genius at spinning a yarn, became the inspiration for creating beloved characters Tom Sawyer and Huckleberry Finn. Let's explore Twain's enchanting Cave State, allowing its Ozark beauty and mystique to flow as easily as the Mississippi River divides the Missouri Ozarks from the tallgrass prairie state of Illinois.

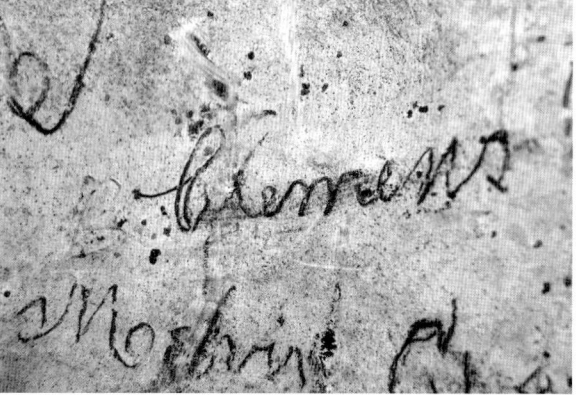

Above: Missouri Ozarks regional map. *Author's collection.*

Left: Clemens's authenticated signature was discovered inside Mark Twain Cave in 2019. *Courtesy of Mark Twain Cave Complex.*

During his formative years in Hannibal (1839–53, ages four to seventeen), Clemens inscribed his name on the cave wall. The cave was later immortalized with publishing *The Adventures of Tom Sawyer* in 1876 and became a tourist destination. The spotlight was again on the cave 166 years after Twain left Hannibal with the discovery of the long sought-after "Clemens" signature. On September 24, 2019, his signature was found in an unlit passageway, bringing the cave celebrity status once again. According to Kevin MacDonnell, a Twain scholar, the author probably attempted to scratch his name and then used a pencil to write on top of it. Scholars MacDonnell and Alan Gribben authenticated the signature.

MISSOURI OZARKS LEGENDS & LORE

MARK TWAIN'S HANNIBAL ROOTS AND THE MARK TWAIN CAVE

300 Cave Hollow Road, Hannibal, MO 63401

Hannibal has had a hard time of it ever since I can recollect, and I was "raised" there. First, it had me for a citizen, but I was too young then to really hurt the place.

—*Mark Twain, letter to the Alta California, dated April 16, 1867, published on May 26, 1867*

The Mark Twain Cave was discovered in the winter of 1819, when Jack Sims tracked a panther into what appeared to be a small den. It was, in fact, an extensive underground network of caves. Mark Twain's boyhood home and museum in Hannibal includes six properties that are listed in the National Register of Historic Places. Two interactive museums and his boyhood home, which was built in the 1840s and opened to the public in 1912, face a cobblestone street that leads to the Mississippi River.

Mark Twain Cave was made famous by the author himself, who grew up in the Mississippi River town of Hannibal, Missouri. As a child, he spent much of his childhood playing in the cave, which was near his home. His fondness for the cave followed him into adulthood, and it eventually became immortalized in his writings. Along with nearby Cameron Cave, it became a registered National Natural Landmark in 1972, with a citation reading, "Exceptionally good examples of the maze type of cavern development." The cave—known as McDougal's Cave back in Twain's day—plays an important role in the novel *The Adventures of Tom Sawyer* (1876) by Mark Twain.

A bat is beautifully soft and silky; I do not know any creature that is pleasanter to the touch or is more grateful for caressings, if offered in the right spirit. I know all about these coleoptera, because our great cave, three miles below Hannibal, was multitudinously stocked with them, and often I brought them home to amuse my mother with. It was easy to manage if it was a school day, because then I had ostensibly been to school and hadn't any bats. She was not a suspicious person, but full of trust and confidence; and when I said, "There's something in my coat pocket for you," she would put her hand in. But she always took it out again, herself; I didn't have to tell her. It was remarkable, the way she couldn't learn to like private bats. The more experience she had, the more she could not change her views.

—*Mark Twain, Autobiography of Mark Twain, 1906*

15

MISSOURI OZARKS LEGENDS & LORE

Mark Twain's boyhood home in Hannibal, Missouri (*second building on the left*), with its nearby cave and Mississippi River setting, is the inspiration for characters Tom Sawyer and Huckleberry Finn. *Courtesy of Visit Hannibal.*

Mark Twain Cave, where the author would collect multitudes of bats to take home to his mother. The more experience she had, the more she couldn't learn to appreciate private bats. *Courtesy of Ruth Ann Hentschke, Extra Innings Photography.*

MISSOURI OZARKS LEGENDS & LORE

Mark Twain Cave tours are a popular experience, lasting about an hour and a half. The natural setting and tour are enhanced by having visitors carry lanterns, as when the cave was explored for the first time in 1925.

Two State Mottos

Missouri has the cultural reputation of having people who find it difficult to make up their minds. Taken to the extreme, Missouri's role in the Civil War involved both Union and Confederate soldiers fighting on both sides. The state was divided right down to its towns and families. Brothers fought against brothers, resulting in Missouri having Union and Confederate dead buried side by side.

Missouri native Kathleen Madigan (from the St. Louis suburb of Ferguson) uses her stand-up comedy to exploit the indecisive nature of Missourians by saying that during the Civil War, we didn't need to leave the state—we could have stayed home and fought one another locally.

Missouri has not just one motto but two, as documented in the *Official Manual of the State of Missouri*.

Official Motto

Missouri's official state motto is *Salus Populi Suprema Lex Esto*, Latin for "The welfare of the people shall be the supreme law," and it is displayed on the official state seal. The official motto is credited to Missouri U.S. Congressman Willard Duncan Vandiver, U.S. House of Representatives, 1897–1903. As a member of the U.S. House Committee on Naval Affairs, Vandiver gave a speech at an 1899 naval banquet in Philadelphia, where he made the declaration, "I come from a state that raises corn and cotton and cockleburs and Democrats, and frothy eloquence neither convinces nor satisfies me. I am from Missouri. You have got to show me."

Unofficial Motto

Missouri's unofficial motto, although more common throughout the state and used on Missouri license plates, is that of the Show Me State. There are a few legends behind the slogan's origin.

17

Missouri Ozarks Legends & Lore

The unofficial motto of Missouri originated in Leadville, Colorado. The phrase was a term of ridicule during a miners' strike during the mid-1890s. Miners from the lead districts of southwest Missouri (Joplin) had been brought in to take the place of strikers. Joplin miners were not familiar with Colorado mining methods and needed schooling. Pit bosses began saying, "That man is from Missouri. You'll have to show him."

The "Show Me" motto branches into two spin-off interpretations. One implies the unwavering judicious character of Missourians. True that. The other, interpreted and understood by natives of the state, is like an inside joke that refers to the abject stubbornness of its people.

Missouri is about as smack-dab in the middle of the country as any state can be. It's bordered by Ohio to the north, Arkansas to the south, Illinois to the east and Kansas to the west. The Ozarks, also known as the Ozark Plateau, covers nearly forty-seven thousand square miles, making it the most extensive highland between the Appalachians and Rockies. The span covers a significant portion of northern Arkansas and most of southern Missouri, plus a section of western Oklahoma and the extreme southeastern corner of Kansas.

The boundary of the Ozark Plateau in southern Missouri is generally defined by the Missouri River to the north, the Mississippi River to the east, the Arkansas River to the south and the Grand and Neosho Rivers to the west. Another way to distinguish the boundary is that it extends from Interstate 40 in central Arkansas (northward) to about Interstate 70 in central Missouri.

The Missouri Ozarks comprise a heavily eroded dome of ancient sedimentary rock where gorge-cut hills and tables present limestone chasms and prairies amid mixed woods, creating some of the best outdoor scenery in the country. With oaks, hickories and shortleaf pines, the Ozarks are evocative of the Appalachians and yet unique by way of rugged forests and dissected plateaus.

The U.S. Forest Service provides protection for areas in the Mark Twain and Ozark–St. Francis National Forests, a rare roadless wilderness that beckons outdoor enthusiasts. Likewise, the Ozark Trail offers more than 360 miles of hiking trails from St. Louis into Arkansas and will eventually form a network that connects with the Arkansas Ozark Highlands Trail.

The Missouri Ozarks provide refuge for wildlife. Once hunted to extinction, American black bears have rebounded to healthy numbers, feeding on nuts and berries and the occasional fawn or feral piglet. Bobcats and coyotes are common, plus the roadrunners and collared lizards that are usually found in the Southwest thrive here.

18

MISSOURI OZARKS LEGENDS & LORE

Geological features consistent with karst topography define the Missouri Ozarks. They are natural springs, losing streams, sinkholes and caves commonly found in the limestone of the Springfield Plateau located in southwest Missouri, and abundant in the dolomite bedrock of the Salem Plateau in the southeast section of the state.

A losing stream is also known as a disappearing stream, influent stream or sinking river. It is defined as a stream or river that loses water as it flows downstream. The water infiltrates into the ground, replenishing local groundwater tables. Losing streams are common in regions of karst topography, where the stream water may be completely captured by a cavern system, becoming a subterranean river. A losing stream is the opposite of a gaining stream, which increases in volume farther downstream as it gains water from local aquifers.

OZARK INTERIOR HIGHLANDS

Of the five physiographic Ozark regions, this book addresses the Salem and Springfield Plateaus, which compose the Missouri Ozarks. The heavily forested plateau is home to more than twenty named rugged state and national forests. Deciduous trees like oak and hickory, plus evergreen shortleaf pines, compose the forests that are evocative of the Appalachians, but with their own Ozark identity by way of dissected plateaus with escarpments, knobs and craggy landforms.

Mark Twain National Forest

The Mark Twain National Forest is a walloping 1.5 million acres of public land of astounding beauty. It is spread out through twenty-nine Missouri counties and promotes a healthy forest that plays a part in maintaining and restoring natural plant and animal species.

With more than 750 miles of trails for hiking, horseback riding and mountain biking, sections of the Ozark Trail wind through the Mark Twain National Forest, which has more than 350 meandering miles of perennial streams suitable for floating, canoeing and kayaking, as well as wilderness camping in rural solitude.

The trail project is expanding in far southeast Missouri near Doniphan, Winona, Van Buren and Poplar Bluff, where more than 100,000 acres are

Missouri Ozarks Legends & Lore

undergoing restoration. Additionally, the Mark Twain National Forest is committed to the eradication of feral swine in Missouri as a member of the Missouri Feral Hog Eradication Partnership.

The Salem Plateau

Named after the town of Salem, Missouri, the Salem Plateau is the largest of the two plateaus that define the Interior Highlands located in southeast Missouri. Formerly an inland sea, it is a heavily eroded dome of ancient dolomite and sedimentary limestone bedrock. Hills and tables feature limestone gorges and prairies amid mixed broad leaf hardwoods to present some of the best scenery in the country.

Also known as the Central Plateau, the Salem Plateau is a broad band across southern Missouri that generally stops at the Mississippi River (to the east) and the Missouri River (to the north). It includes the city of St. Louis, plus numerous river towns along the Mississippi as it flows south toward Memphis.

The Springfield Plateau

Named after the city of Springfield, Missouri, the Springfield Plateau is the second largest of the two plateaus that encompass the Interior Highlands. Located in the southwestern section of the state, the Springfield Plateau differs from the Salem Plateau in that is consists mainly of sedimentary limestone bedrock. The Springfield Plateau in southwest Missouri includes the cities of Springfield, Joplin and Branson.

Early Settlers

The earliest Missouri Ozark settlers came from France, followed by the Scotch-Irish, who had originally settled in the southern Appalachians and then came to Missouri Ozarks during westward expansion to work in the mines. Likewise, German craftsmen came to Missouri as artisan builders during the early 1800s. The term *Ozark* refers not only to mountains but also to the melding of cultures, architecture and dialect shared by people who live on the Interior Highland plateau. Much of the Ozark population is of

English, Scotch-Irish and German descent, and regional culture is derived from those families who settled the Ozarks and have remained in the area since the early 1800s.

Cities and towns in the Ozark Salem Plateau that are profiled in the following narrative are listed by the counties in which they are located. They are Iron, Madison, New Madrid, Oregon, Reynolds, Shannon, St. Francois, Ste. Genevieve, Oregon and Warren Counties—with the exception of St. Louis (city and country).

OZARK ENGLISH

A dialect called "Ozark English" is spoken in northwestern Arkansas and southern Missouri that is unique to the Ozark Mountains. It's a relative of the Scotch-Irish dialect spoken in the Appalachian Mountains and exists in the Ozarks as the result of Scotch-Irish migration from Appalachia beginning in the late 1830s.

Geographic location and consequent isolation in the Ozark Mountains allowed preservation of the archaic dialect spoken by Appalachian settlers. The isolation fostered development of the dialect that sets Ozark English apart from standard American English. Like its Appalachian cousin, Ozark English is linked to stereotypes that mistakenly depict the Ozark mountain culture as backward, and the reason why will surprise you.

Scholars began relating Ozark English to older forms of English as early as the 1890s, and linking similarities between Ozark speech, words and phrases found in English literature from the Middle Ages, as well as Elizabethan and Shakespearean literary periods.

There are no people who are quite so vulgar as the over-refined.
—*Mark Twain*

In the twentieth century, researchers studied language in remote communities in the Ozarks, documenting various archaic words and usages. Charles Morrow Wilson, a Fayetteville, Arkansas native, and Vance Randolph (author of *Ozark Magic and Folklore*), a seminal figure in Ozark folklore studies, were among the scholars studying Ozark English during this period. Wilson spent time with residents of Hemmed-in-Holler (Newton County) during the Great Depression. He found that the speakers of Ozark English were hypothetically capable of swapping talk and breaking bread

Missouri Ozarks Legends & Lore

with farmers of Chaucer's England and would experience few linguistic misunderstandings. Wilson recorded that an Ozarker "tarries" to pass time and "carries a budget on his back," just as Shakespeare's characters did. Randolph published several works on the Ozark dialect, many of which appeared in revised forms in *Down in the Holler* (1953), a collaboration with George P. Wilson, which explores various aspects of Ozark English, including its pronunciation, grammar and vocabulary. Like Wilson, Randolph recorded instances in which Ozarker pronunciation reflected earlier English, words such as *heerd*, *deef*, *sheath*, *chimley* and *anyways*.

In 1988, researchers Donna Christian, Walt Wolfram and Nanjo Dube published a study of Ozark English as part of a larger project to enhance existing linguistic studies through a comparison of Ozark English and Appalachian English.

A fieldwork group led by Dube documented properties in Ozark English, including the completive *done*, *a-* prefixing, irregular verbs and aspects of subject-verb agreement. The team studied the completive *done* (as in "I done told you") and concluded that it appears almost exclusively in speech of those over fifty years of age. *A-* prefixing occurs in front of verbs, such as "He just kept a-tryin' and a-cryin' and a-wantin' to come out." Again, researchers observed fewer instances in younger speakers. The goal was to assert the Elizabethan influences that exist in isolated communities within the region, while acknowledging the changes in the speech of younger Ozarkers.

Ozark English—once fostered by regional Show Me geographic location and isolation from outside influence—has today become a fusion of the old and new, a unique dialect born of a people's cultural history.

Chapter 2

OZARK SALEM PLATEAU CAVES

The mystery of karst earth elements existed millennia in total darkness and silence, as water seeped through sedimentary bedrock over millions of years to sculpt the landscape. Karst topography is evident in a landscape that is characterized by caves, sinkholes, fissures and underground streams. Surface streams are usually absent in regions where there is plenty of rainfall, where carbonate-rich bedrock—such as limestone, gypsum or dolomite—is easily dissolved.

Such is the Missouri Ozarks, which is broken down into two areas. They are the Salem and Springfield Plateaus, defined by geological features such as gently rolling hills separated by steep escarpments that dramatically interrupt the hills.

Differences in the plateaus relate to the rock type. While the Salem Plateau is made of older dolomites, limestones and sandstones, the Springfield Plateau is primarily limestone and chert. The Springfield Plateau drains through wide, mature streams, ultimately feeding the White River, while the Salem Plateau drains mostly into aquifers.

The Salem Plateau, consisting of sedimentary bedrock, has the additional feature of the St. Francois Mountains, which are of volcanic origin. Essentially, the igneous rock of St. Francois Mountains is older, and the sedimentary bedrock of the plateau formed around them.

MISSOURI OZARKS LEGENDS & LORE

CRAWFORD COUNTY:
LEASBURG, ONONDAGA CAVE STATE PARK

7556 Highway H, Leasburg, MO 65535

The area around the National Natural Landmark on the Meramec River known as Onondaga Cave was settled in 1850. The cave, known as Mammoth Cave of Missouri, was discovered later in 1886. At that time, area caves were being mined for cave onyx, used in architectural applications, but Mammoth Cave of Missouri was spared that fate thanks to the Louisiana Purchase Exposition for the 1904 World's Fair in St. Louis. The cave was renamed Onondaga Cave for an Iroquois tribe, with the translation meaning "People of the Mountain."

When it was discovered that about half of Onondaga Cave was under privately owned land, an additional tunnel entrance was commissioned, and an underground fence was erected in the cave at the property line. The second half of the cave became known as the Missouri Caverns.

When then candidate Harry S Truman and members of his Democratic Party visited Missouri Caverns, Republican party members were also there for a tour of Onondaga Cave. Like exemplary politicians, the two parties met at the underground fence separating the caves and engaged in a political debate.

After a time of decreased interest in tourism during the two world wars, electrification of the rural Missouri Ozarks allowed the entire cave to be wired for lighting, and the old tour paths and stairs and bridges were updated. This initiated a time of prosperity for the caverns. An advertising campaign ensured that celebrities visited the caverns, and by 1954, church services and wedding ceremonies were taking place in the cave.

Currently, walking tours of Onondaga Cave take visitors through well-lit one-mile-long paved walkways, where guides draw attention to geological features such as the Twins and King's Canopy, along with dripping stalactites, massive stalagmites, active flowstones and other speleothems. A river flows slowly through the cave. Outside, the park offers access to the Meramec River via the Vilander Bluff Natural Area.

24

MISSOURI OZARKS LEGENDS & LORE

FRANKLIN COUNTY: STANTON, MERAMEC CAVERNS STATE PARK

I-44 West, Exit 230, Stanton, MO 63079

Meramec Caverns State Park is listed in the National Register of Historic Places. This amazing Ozark setting along the Meramec River is defined by limestone cliffs and hardwood forests and is home to forty caves. All of this natural wonder is bordered by historic Route 66 west of St. Louis.

The Meramec River, at 218 miles long, is one of the longest free-flowing waterways in Missouri, and the cavern is one of the world's largest cave formations and the largest commercial cave in Missouri. If ever a cave had a colorful history, Meramec Cavern is it. It sheltered Native Americans for centuries before French colonial miners exploited it for minerals. Then, during the Civil War, saltpeter from the cave was used to manufacture gunpowder, and the notorious outlaw Jesse James hid out in the cavern during the 1870s.

Fascinating formations in Meramec Caverns—such as the Stage Curtain, Underground River, an ancient natural limestone formation known as the

The Meramec River near Meramec Caverns State Park in 2021, when ice formed on the river bluff. *Courtesy of Ruth Ann Hentschke, Extra Innings Photography.*

25

Meramec Caverns features 4.6 miles of caves and an underground river alongside historic Route 66 in Stanton, Missouri. *Courtesy of Wikimedia Commons.*

Wine Table and a seven-story natural cave that is known as the Mansion—are all highlighted on guided tours by rangers. With more than forty caves in the park, the most fascinating is Fisher Cave, with its low, narrow passages along streams that lead to massive underground rooms filled with calcite deposits and thirty-foot-tall helictite columns. Along the path, you'll see ancient bear claw marks on some walls.

In 1927, the extended network was discovered, revealing the present 4.6 miles. The cave was introduced to the public as a tourist attraction in 1935 by Lester B. Dill, who invented the bumper sticker as a means of promoting the caverns. Guided seasonal tours are offered by the park's naturalists.

CAMDEN COUNTY: CAMDENTON, BRIDAL CAVE

526 Bridal Cave Road, Camdenton, MO 65020-2814

The idea of getting married in a cave might sound bizarre until you see the magnificent Bridal Cave near the Lake of the Ozarks. Located just outside the town of Camdenton, the cave beneath Thunder Mountain holds the legend of the marriage of a native couple that took place centuries ago in the cave. Bridal Cave is branded as one of the most beautiful caves in the country, with giant columns, stalactites, stalagmites, Mystery Lake and many other underground geological formations. For those who are not seeking nuptials, there are regular guided tours.

ST. LOUIS CITY: FOUR LIVING URBAN CAVES

Cherokee Cave

Cherokee Cave is a karst living urban cave. It formed more than 1 million years ago when acidic rainwater seeped into small cracks and fissures in the limestone bedrock. Over time, the acid began to eat away at the limestone, creating small channels that soon became larger channels as water accelerated the process to form the cave.

Cherokee Cave is located in south St. Louis, near the Mississippi River. Specifically, it is beneath the historic Benton Park neighborhood, meaning red brick and brownstone flats are located right on top of the cave.

MISSOURI OZARKS LEGENDS & LORE

Vintage Cherokee Cave postcard. *Courtesy of Chatillon-DeMenil House Foundation.*

Cherokee Cave is laden with history and legend, ranging from its use by Native Americans to its role as part of the Underground Railroad and its connection to area mansions where the rich and famous once accessed the cave by way of the Lemp mansion spiral staircase that led to an underground swimming pool and theater.

English Cave

English Cave, located fifty feet below Benton Park, was simply forgotten when Prohibition killed the beer industry. Entrances to the cave were closed, and it was only a matter of time before nobody living remembered where they were located, according to United Press International. Historically, the cave was used for storing beer in the early 1800s. In fact, nearby Lemp Brewery had been the epicenter of the city because of English and Cherokee Caves. Before refrigeration was available, underground storage in caves was a year-round viable option, with a continuous temperature of fifty-six degrees. English Cave was lost from memory for more than one hundred years, but it has been rediscovered underneath Benton Park. The legendary cave has been used for storing ale and has been a mushroom farm, a wine grotto and community gathering place at different times.

A research team drilled down about fifty feet from ground level—the drilling location being a lucky guess—right through the limestone ceiling into the cave. The team then lowered cameras and a LIDAR unit map into the cave and determined its size as being about thirty by fifteen feet and seven and a half feet tall.

When the small lake at Benton Park was constructed, the water drained out several times. It was determined that was water was seeping into an underground cave. The lake was then lined with concrete. Problem solved.

Lemp Cave

Like the others, Lemp Cave is the result of sedimentary rock that formed when the Ozarks were an inland sea. Also located in Benton Park, a large section of the cave, purchased by Adam Lemp in 1845, was designated for storage and lagering. Adam's son, William, took over the operation in 1862 and built a large brewery complex directly over the site of the cave.

The Lemp sections of the cave were altered for industrial use. A series of lagering rooms are separated from others via masonry walls with large arched doorways. Brick trenches in the floor drain the excess water from the cave, and ice holes in the ceiling accommodated large blocks of ice that cooled the cave to the appropriate temperature for aging German lager. In later years, the Lemp family used the caves as a source of entertainment by means of the theater and heated pool under the mansion in Benton Park.

When the Eighteenth Amendment to the Constitution was ratified in 1919 (prohibiting the sale of alcohol), the Lemp Brewery floundered. The International Shoe Company purchased it in 1922, but little was heard about the caves until 1950, when they were opened as a tourist attraction.

Minnehaha Cave

Minnehaha Cave, another result of karst topography, is also located under Benton Park below what is now the corner of Broadway and Cherokee Street, with Broadway paralleling the Mississippi River.

In 1945, Lee Hess purchased the DeMenil Mansion and a building at the corner of Broadway and Cherokee Street that stood over the original

Missouri Ozarks Legends & Lore

entrance to the Minnehaha Cave, intending to turn the defunct brewery cave into a tourist attraction. The cave was filled with clay and sediment that had washed into it over the centuries. When his plan to feature natural cave rock required excavating the clay sediment, a large deposit of animal bones was discovered. The American Museum of Natural History determined them to be the skulls of a prehistoric pig called a peccary (*Platygonus compressus*). Soon, more than three thousand fossils were catalogued, as reported by the *Missouri Speleology Journal*.

When the Missouri Highway Department purchased the property from Hess in 1961, construction of I-55 collapsed a portion of the cave, including the museum entrance. Most of it remains intact but is inaccessible to the public.

Shannon County: Salem, Devils Well

The cave known as Devils Well is an unusual karst window, allowing visitors to have a look deep into a sinkhole that was created when the roof of this huge cavern collapsed. This formed the large sinkhole with another hole in the bottom, through which it is possible to see the largest underground lake in the state. A spiral staircase makes viewing the lake easier, at least for the agile visitor. The low-lying riparian zone has shallow soil, rocky ridges and deep swales. It is a part of the Ozark National Scenic Riverways and can be viewed by the public any day during daylight hours.

Devils Well is located near Akers just off Route KK, and the road leading to the cave is steep and rough. Entrance is free, and there is a light in the stairwell that visitors can activate themselves. Outside the cave, a 4.6-mile-long trail leads from Devils Well to Cave Spring. From the trail, you can see the path of the water from Devils Well.

Chapter 3

OZARK SPRINGFIELD PLATEAU CAVES

CAMDEN COUNTY: CAMDEN, OZARK CAVERNS

Lake of the Ozarks State Park, Camden, MO

Located in the Lake of the Ozarks State Park, Ozark Caverns can only be explored by carrying a lantern since there is no electricity. The first geological formation visitors see is Angel Showers, a perpetual water shower dripping from the rock high above. Another fascinating feature is a wall of clay with bear claw marks that are centuries old. The cave is home to salamanders, four species of bats and sixteen species of invertebrates. Toward the end of the cave, there is a wall where visitors have left their signatures since the 1800s. An information center and museum with artifacts and information on Missouri caves and parks is just outside the cave. The website vacationidea.com cites this as being among Missouri's best caves.

CHRISTIAN COUNTY: SPRINGFIELD, SMALLIN CIVIL WAR CAVE

4872 North Farm Road 125, Springfield, MO 65803

Smallin Civil War Cave, documented in 1818 by Henry Rowe Schoolcraft, holds a treasure-trove of Civil War history and is now listed in the National

Smallin Civil War Cave, listed in the National Register as a historic district, holds a treasure-trove of Civil War history. *Courtesy of Smallin Civil War Cave.*

Register as a historic district. The cave entrance is fifty-five feet tall and one hundred feet wide. The wild cave tours are two-hour one-mile underground off-the-beaten-path adventures lit only by the headlamp on your helmet. You'll walk through water at least two feet deep and fifty-four degrees in temperature and navigate rugged terrain. Civil War Lantern Tours are offered in the fall. One-hour (accessible) guided tours span the distance of one half mile and are wheelchair and stroller accessible.

GREENE COUNTY, CAMDEN, FANTASTIC CAVERNS

4872 North Farm Road 125, Springfield, MO 65803

Discovered in 1862 by a farmer named John Knox (and his dog, name unknown), the cave that would come to be known as Fantastic Caverns has a unique history and a story as fantastic as its dark twists and turns.

Because it was during the Civil War, Knox knew that he had to keep his discovery secret in order to protect the saltpeter reserve. Saltpeter is a white powder that exists naturally in some caves and can be used to make gunpowder. Had the Confederate army known of the saltpeter, it might have used it to produce gunpowder, so he waited until after the war had ended to make his find public news. The cave wasn't explored until 1867.

Knox put out an advertisement in 1867 in the Springfield newspaper for explorers to investigate the cave. A team of twelve women from the Springfield Women's Athletic Club responded and went into the uncharted cavern with ropes and lanterns, mapping the cave and establishing themselves as local legends. Their names are carved in the cave's interior walls, bolstering their part in the history of the great caverns.

During Prohibition, according to Atlas Obscura, the cave was used as a speakeasy. Then, during the 1950s, the cave gained the title "Fantastic Caverns" and a reputation as a well-regarded concert hall. The caves are today privately owned and are open to the public. Tours are conducted in jeep-drawn trams to protect the fragile environment and allow tourists to enjoy the visit in comfort. The fifty-five-minute tour goes along a wide, well-lit path, a former riverbed surrounded by huge formations such as stalactites, stalagmites, soda straws, cave pearls, flowstones and massive columns.

MISSOURI OZARKS LEGENDS & LORE

Springfield, Riverbluff Cave

2327 West Farm Road 190, Springfield, MO 65810

Riverbluff Cave, a paleontological site near Springfield, Missouri, is full of fascinating stalactites, columns and stalagmites. Workers blasting for a new road accidentally discovered the cave on September 11, 2001. While most people were watching replays of planes colliding into the World Trade Center Towers, road construction crews were colliding into something of their own on that fateful September day.

The cave is noted as karst landscape of the Ozark Mountains and Springfield Plateau, as well as of Mississippian limestone that is made up of marine limestone and is common in the region. Riverbluff Cave is about 830,000 years old and is the oldest fossil cave in the United States, a time capsule of the ice age. It features Pleistocene fossils, the most significant being that of the short-faced bear, the largest species of bear on Earth at about six feet tall and weighing 1,400 pounds.

Although Riverbluff Cave isn't open to the public, it offers virtual tours, plus the Riverbluff Cave Field House opened in 2009 to show fossils from the cave and other sites around the world.

McDONALD COUNTY: NOEL, BLUFF DWELLERS CAVE

163 Cave Road, McDonald County, Noel, MO 64854

In 1925, Bluff Dwellers Cave was discovered when Mr. C. Arthur Browning was checking animal traps on his family's property and noticed a cool breeze coming from a limestone outcrop. Exploring a small cavity led to locating two natural openings by removing loose rock and debris and then large slabs of limestone that concealed the cave.

Mr. Browning was in his forties when he made the discovery, and he was astonished to find a cave so large and intricate on land where he'd lived his entire life. Within two years, Bluff Dwellers Cave was opened to the public for tours, and the cave is currently owned and operated by the grandchildren of Arthur Browning.

Bluff Dwellers Cave is an archaeologically significant cave with about four thousand feet of explored passages. It's located in the Ozark Mountains near Noel, McDonald County, Missouri, along the Elk River, at the Missouri southwestern border close to Fayetteville, Arkansas.

What makes Bluff Dwellers Cave archaeologically significant is that Paleoindians, called Bluff Dwellers, lived in the caves some twelve thousand years ago. This lends itself to excavation and the study of artifacts and other physical remains. Like so many caves in the Ozarks, Bluff Dwellers formed during the Paleozoic era from water seeping through the cracks and joints in the St. Joe Limestone. Notably, St. Joe Limestone is a formation specific to northern Arkansas, southern Missouri and northeastern Oklahoma. It preserves fossils, such as crinoids, brachiopods, bryozoa, conodonts, blastoids, ostracods and rugose coral.

Bluff Dwellers Cave has formations (speleothems) shaped by deposits of minerals from water, such as lily pads and cave corals. The crown jewel formations of the cave are the Musical Chimes, which are curtains of hollow rock stalactites that have musical frequency similar to a xylophone. Also notable are the Ten Ton Balanced Rock on two pivots, and the rimstone pool. The cave is home to albino cave crayfish, grotto salamanders and the eastern pipistrelle bat.

BRANSON, TANEY COUNTY

The Ozark tourist mecca of Branson, Missouri, has something for everyone and has become a popular destination for vacationers from all around the country. From live music to an amusement venue and cave tours; from Table Rock Lake's water sports to a cruise aboard the showboat *Branson Bell*; and from shopping to ghost tours, Branson has it all and offers lodging from rustic to hoity-toity.

Branson, Silver Dollar City and Marvel Cave

399 Indian Point Road, Silver Dollar City, HCR 1 Box 791, Branson, MO 65616

This internationally awarded 1880s-style theme park features more than forty exciting rides amid sixty-one acres of quaint Ozark terrain and offers visitors access to Marvel Cave.

Marvel Cave is a National Natural Landmark located in the Springfield Plateau, west of Branson, Missouri. It is accessible from the top of Roark

Mountain in Stone County at Silver Dollar City. As early as the 1500s, Osage Indians knew about the cave after a tribe member fell through a karst sinkhole, which is now the cave's main entrance, located inside Silver Dollar City, Branson. The cave opened as a show cave in 1894. Within its five-hundred-foot depth, flowstone, stalagmites and stalactites are found. It's part of Silver Dollar City, and it has the largest cave entrance of not only all caves in the country but also in the world.

Marvel Cave was regarded with superstitious awe by the old-timers, who noticed a subterranean cat room full of panther and bobcat bones. An old story claims that animals from miles around made their way to the cavern to die there, leaving their body with those of their ancestors. The old-timers would warn tourists away from the cave for their own protection.

The entrance, labeled the Cathedral Room, measures 204 feet high, 225 feet wide and 411 feet long. The cave is the deepest in Missouri at 505 feet. Visitors enter through an overhead opening and then descend a winding stairway to the bottom 94 feet below. There are two kinds of tours. The most popular, the Traditional Cave Tour, moves along well-lit concrete paths with a guide. Its six hundred stairs descend 500 feet below the surface during the course of the tour, and then a cable car takes the group back to the surface. The second tour is the Lantern Cave Tour, where visitors use lanterns for lighting, rather than electricity, and have access through cave sections that are restricted to other visitors.

Branson's Three Lakes

Table Rock Lake, with clear, fresh water, is a Branson jewel. The man-made reservoir spans more than forty-three thousand acres that create 750 miles of shoreline in Missouri and Arkansas. Water sports like boating and swimming are popular in this stunning Ozark landscape.

Lake Taneycomo formed when the White River was dammed in order to create the reservoir now known as Table Rock Lake. The river below Table Rock transitioned into a lake after the White River was tamed. Taneycomo's twenty-two-mile stretch of water covers 2,080 surface acres and runs from Branson to Forsyth's Powersite Dam. Lake Taneycomo has made Branson famous for trout fishing.

MISSOURI OZARKS LEGENDS & LORE

Table Rock Lake (reservoir) is a Branson jewel that comprises forty-three thousand acres of water and 750 miles of shoreline. *Courtesy of Wikimedia Commons, KTrimble.*

Bull Shoals Lake begins where Lake Taneycomo meets Powersite Dam. The less populated Bull Shoals Lake spans forty-five thousand acres of Missouri Ozarks and offers nearly one thousand miles of shoreline amid hardwood forests; it is known for bass fishing and water sports.

Chapter 4

MISSOURI OZARKS TRAILS

OZARK TRAIL

The Missouri Ozarks Trail is still being developed for hiking, biking and equestrian recreation. It will eventually span about five hundred miles from St. Louis in a southwest direction to meet with the Arkansas Trail. When joined with the Ozark Highlands Trail in Arkansas, the full hiking distance from end to end will be about seven hundred miles. In addition, an independent loop trail will go through the St. Francois Mountains in Iron County, Missouri.

The trail is composed of thirteen joined sections that vary in length from 8 to 40 miles. The longest continuous stretch available for hiking is 225 miles, from Onondaga Cave State Park to the Eleven Point River. When hiking the trail in sections, prearranged shuttles are available to pick you up and deliver you to the next location.

The best way to use the shuttle is to park your vehicle where you plan to end your hike and then catch a shuttle back to where you wish to begin. By doing that, you can take your time and not have to worry about getting a shuttle at the end of your hike to get back to your vehicle.

MISSOURI OZARKS LEGENDS & LORE

Ozark Mountains seen in the distance along the Katy Trail. *Courtesy of Ruth Ann Hentschke, Extra Innings Photography.*

KATY TRAIL

A railroad is like a lie you have to keep building to make it stand.

—*Mark Twain*

The Katy Trail is the repurposed corridor of the former Missouri-Kansas-Texas (MKT) Railroad, better known as the Katy. The railroad was established in 1865, and then 1870 its name changed to MKT Railroad, as it had the intention to be the first railway to connect the great state of Texas to the rest of the country.

When the railroad retired the route in 1986, the Missouri State Parks Department acquired the right-of-way and then began constructing the Katy Trail Park in 1987. The first section opened in 1990 at Rocheport, Missouri. Over the years, more stretches were added until the 238-mile trail was complete, making it a favorite natural destination. Its crushed limestone surface allows bicyclists to easily take in the miles, enjoy magnificent Ozark views and explore small-town history along the way.

Seasonal changes augment the inherent personality of the Katy, which remains open all year long. Missouri offers four distinct seasons in which to explore. Spring's mild temperatures bring about dogwood and redbud blooming trees; summer offers forest and rolling farmland views; and the fall

39

Missouri Ozarks Legends & Lore

foliage along the Missouri river bluffs is an array of jaw-dropping colors in red, orange and yellow. As for winter's offering, well, you're on your own to chart the winter beauty of the Katy Trail.

You can travel at your own pace or customize your trip itinerary anywhere from a day ride to a weeklong adventure. The 238 mile trail spans the state. It runs along the Missouri River that skirts the northern border of the Missouri Ozarks Salem Plateau. Now, that's a lot to expect from the seat of a bicycle, yet the Ozark Katy Trail delivers. This longest continuous rail-trail in the country gives new credence to the term "road trip," as it guides the traveler from St. Charles County (near St. Louis) to Clinton, Missouri, which is about 76 miles southeast of Kansas City. Imagine going that distance without a Rand-McNally!

The Katy brought new life to many small declining river towns along the path that parallels the Missouri River when they began offering accommodations and services for hikers and bikers by way of services like B&Bs and restaurants. For a complete guide to the Katy's trailhead stops, see katytrailmo.com/katy-trail-maps. Listed here are some of the favorite stops.

Katy Trail Head Stops

The trail either begins or ends at Machens, the eastern end of the trail, depending on what direction you are headed. Headed west, your first stop is St. Charles, Missouri, one of the most historic towns along the route.

ST. CHARLES COUNTY: ST. CHARLES

St. Charles, founded in 1769 by Louis Blanchette, is one of the earliest settlements on the Missouri River. A French settlement, its original name (*Les Petites Côtes*) translated means "The Little Hills." It gained its place in history when Meriwether Lewis and William Clark began what we know as the Lewis and Clark Expedition from this site in May 1804. After their return in 1806, the town was renamed St. Charles. The city of St. Charles is the county seat of St. Charles County and was the state's first capital (1821–26) before it was moved to Jefferson City. The eastern Missouri city sits on bluffs that overlook the Missouri River. It is located about twenty-two miles west of St. Louis, before the Missouri meets the Mississippi River just north of St. Louis.

Headed west from the trail's origin in Machens, the first stop at mile marker 12.5 is St. Charles. The city's charming downtown historic district is known for its red brick buildings that house tempting shops, boutiques, cafés

MISSOURI OZARKS LEGENDS & LORE

and coffee shops set amid scenic Missouri River views. This river town is a perfect trailhead stop along the Katy, with limestone bluffs bordering the trail through Weldon Spring Wildlife area. This trailhead has added appeal as a good destination day trip for beginners. Bike services and rentals, as well as food and lodging among historic buildings along the river bluffs overlooking the Missouri River, are classic Ozark experiences.

St. Charles County: Defiance, Missouri

At mile marker 32, the trailhead at Defiance features the town that, in authentic Show Me spirit, earned its name by building a depot in 1894 to lure the railroad stop away from nearby Augusta.

Defiance is where the frontiersman Daniel Boone settled. His stone farmhouse is located here and open for tours. Trailhead services include food and lodging and trail supplies.

It's noteworthy that when you reach Defiance, you're entering Missouri wine country. Wouldn't it be fun to take a two-mile detour into, say, Chandler Hill Winery to sample the nectar of the Ozark wine gods as you move through Missouri's Rhineland?

St. Charles County: Augusta, Missouri

The Klondike Quarry area east of Augusta exhibits a particularly fine exposure of St. Peter sandstone. This white quartz sandstone was ground up at this site for use in manufacturing glass.

At mile marker 39.5, the trailhead at Augusta makes a terrific day trip destination from the beginning of the Katy at Machens. The town of Augusta was settled in 1836 on the bluffs overlooking the Missouri River and became a center of German cultural traditions. The Germans established vineyards, and many wineries still thrive today. The section of trail connecting Augusta, Marthasville and Hermann is the heart of an area known as Missouri's Rhineland because of the number of Germans who flocked to this part of the state in the mid-1800s.

My personal recommendation is Mount Pleasant Estates Winery, with its views of the Missouri River Valley from prominent bluffs. Trail users approaching Augusta from the east will see river bluffs of dolomite and sandstone.

Check out the Appellation Café, with outdoor tables overlooking the river valley. Not to be missed is the brick arched vault storage where wine ages underground in oak barrels. You'd be hard-pressed to top the ambiance of Mount Pleasant Estates Winery.

41

Missouri Ozarks Legends & Lore

The river bluff views from Augusta are sweeping and scenic. This, plus historic homes, boutiques, antiques shops, and two wineries make it a desirable stop. The full range of services can be found in Augusta. There are elaborate plans to develop this area, making it a destination to rival Napa Valley.

GASCONADE COUNTY: HERMANN, MISSOURI

At mile marker 76.1, the trailhead at Hermann, Missouri, is another must-see stop. Hermann is one of the most beautiful river towns you'll find anywhere, with its scenic river bluffs and rolling fields. The charming river town is home to a historic downtown, historic homes and churches and wineries. You'll find abundant services here, including lodging, shops, cafés and riverside B&Bs. One added appeal is that Hermann is an Amtrak stop. If you decide to conclude your trip in the historic Ozark town of Hermann and head back toward St. Louis, you can hop the train and, for a nominal fee, take your bike aboard. Chances are you'll have a hard time leaving. It's just that beautiful!

CALLAWAY AND COLE COUNTIES: JEFFERSON CITY, MISSOURI

By the time you hit Jefferson City, you will have traveled 116.5 miles and will have arrived at the Missouri state capitol. You can tour the capitol or take in the state history museum. You'll find abundant services regarding food and lodging.

BOON COUNTY: ROCHEPORT, MISSOURI

At mile marker 152, the trailhead at the tiny hamlet of Rocheport, Missouri, population 240, offers up some shops and galleries for bikers. Services include lodging and food. If Rocheport is an overnight destination, nearby Les Bourgeois Vineyards is great for sipping wine among stunning river views. Throughout Rocheport's spectacular bluffs are rock drawings or pictographs left by Native Americans that merited mention in the journals of Lewis and Clark as they made their way up the Missouri River. A rare surviving pictograph can be seen above Lewis and Clark Cave on the trail. The town of Rocheport has not only many houses that date from before the Civil War but also the only tunnel on the trail. Built around 1893, the stone arched tunnel is 243 feet long.

COOPER COUNTY: BOONVILLE, MISSOURI

Moving right along, mile marker 165 delivers you to Boonville, the county seat of Cooper County, Missouri, with its more than 450 sites in the National

Right: Former train bridge at Gasconade County near Hermann, Missouri, on the Katy Trail. *Courtesy of Ruth Ann Hentschke, Extra Innings Photography.*

Below: Rocheport has the only tunnel on the 1893 repurposed railroad line. The arched tunnel, formerly used by trains, is 243 feet long. *Courtesy of Ruth Ann Hentschke, Extra Innings Photography.*

MISSOURI OZARKS LEGENDS & LORE

Register. Once a major river port, Boonville transitioned into a booming railroad town. Boonville's restored historic depot is the only surviving Spanish Mission–style depot on the trail and has been listed in the National Register since 1990. The depot now serves as the Boonville Chamber of Commerce and visitors' center. Another Boonville attraction is the majestic Budweiser Clydesdales seen at Warm Springs Ranch.

From Boonville, the Katy parallels the path of the Missouri River, where many scenic stretches have towering river bluffs. If you're feeling lucky after 191 miles on the Katy (and who wouldn't be?), consider booking a room for a fun night at the Isle of Capri Casino.

BOONE COUNTY: COLUMBIA, *BOATHENGE*

At first glance, *BoatHenge* (at mile marker 169.9) may seem like nothing more than a bunch of boats turned up on their ends and stuck into Missouri River bottomland. And well, that's exactly what it is to those who look no further. To appreciate the installation, once must travel back in time to, say, 1993 and the advent of the Great Flood, also known as the Hundred Years' Flood, when the boats mysteriously appeared.

According to the *BoatHenge* official website, the circle of marooned dinghies offers a creation story claiming that the work of art either spontaneously sprouted from the earth or fell from the sky on the first day of spring.

A circle of marooned dinghies, known as *BoatHenge*, stand on end alongside the Missouri River in Columbia, accompanied by a legendary creation story. *Courtesy of Ruth Ann Hentschke, Extra Innings Photography.*

Missouri Ozarks Legends & Lore

The creation's nuts-and-bolts reveal six fiberglass boats erupting vertically from the ground in a semi-lunar formation; their height, width and depth planted into the earth average to exactly match that of the original, ancient and mysterious Stonehenge located at Wiltshire, England.

This installation, whether sprouted or fallen, is the work of a group of anonymous artists, and like other installations of a similar vein, it is only by letting the art flow over you that its magic can manifest.

Getting to *BoatHenge* is easy. Follow directions to Coopers Landing, and then *BoatHenge* is just west of there, on the other side of the bridge, visible from the roadside. It is also a stop on the Katy Trail.

Pettis County: Sedalia, Missouri

Mile marker 202 brings you to Sedalia, Missouri. This section transitions from the Osage Plains to the Ozark borderlands, where rolling terrain landscapes span from pasture to deep woods to river bottoms.

Sedalia's historic Katy Depot features Romanesque Revival architecture. Architect Bradford Lee Gilbert designed the depot, which George Goodlander built of limestone from the nearby Georgetown Quarry. The Missouri-Kansas-Texas Railroad began operating in Sedalia in 1873. It was officially opened on May 10, 1896. The popular gathering spot served the

Amtrak delivers Katy Trail hikers/bikers to Sedalia, who then navigate the trail 170 miles back east toward St. Charles, Missouri. *Courtesy of Ruth Ann Hentschke, Extra Innings Photography.*

Missouri Ozarks Legends & Lore

community with elegance and charm for more than sixty years until the last passenger train left the depot in 1958.

From 1998 to 2001, the depot underwent extensive renovation that restored the building to its original grandeur. Now listed in the National Register of Historic Places, the depot is home to Sedalia's Welcome Center. If your timing agrees, visit the Missouri State Fair. Check out the historic downtown district or head over to the Daum Museum of Contemporary Art, which exhibits Warhol, Chihuly and Frankenthaler, among others. The restored MKT depot, one of the largest depots between Kansas City and St. Louis, operates as the Katy Depot Heritage Site.

The Bothwell Lodge State Historic Site has lodging available at the Hotel Bothwell and spa. Time to book a massage and pedicure at trail's end, no doubt! You know you deserve it!

The Katy ends at mile 238 in Clinton, Missouri—76 miles outside Kansas City.

Chapter 5

OZARK FOLKLORE

I find that, as a rule, when a thing is a wonder to us it is not because of what we see in it, but because of what others have seen in it.
We get almost all our wonders second hand.
—*Mark Twain, Following the Equator*

ance Rudolph's book *Ozark Magic and Folklore* is the best resource for authentic Ozark folklore, featuring the inside story on the topics mentioned in the following narrative. Rudolph moved to the Ozarks to study cultural customs as told by native Ozarkers and made some eye-opening and thought-provoking discoveries.

ANIMALS

In Oregon County, near Grand Gulf Park (also known as Missouri's Grand Canyon), early settlers saw a white buck in the woods over a period of time spanning about fifteen years but wouldn't shoot for fear of bad luck. Ozark old-timers won't kill a deer on Sunday, because it's sinful. If they do it anyway, they'll not get another for seven weeks.

Some believe that a fox can charm a squirrel out of a tree by rolling around on the ground beneath it. They believe that the squirrel will become dizzy and fall from the tree.

And did you know that it's bad luck for a rabbit to cross your path from left to right. If that happens, the curse can be removed by slightly tearing an article of your clothing. But if the rabbit crosses your path twice, you are urgently needed at home.

BIRDS

Whatever a man is doing when he hears the first dove of the season is what he'll have to do all summer.

A buzzard will vomit on a person guilty of incest.

In Jasper County (near Joplin), turkey hunters claim that thunder kills birds in the egg. When a powder works blew up over Jasper County, no quail eggs were hatched that year for eight miles around.

BURIAL

Rainy weather at a funeral is the best possible omen, as it's an indication the deceased's soul is at rest. And for goodness sakes, never count the vehicles at a funeral because it foreshadows your own early death.

An Irish funeral tradition is to pause the procession and turn the coffin around so as to confuse the spirit of the deceased and prohibit it from finding its way back home.

COURTSHIP AND MARRIAGE

Girls create love charms by tying little pieces of cloth to the branches of pawpaw or hawthorn trees. If a man hides a dried tongue of a turtle dove in a girl's cabin, she will fall madly in love with him. Putting salt in a fire for seven consecutive days will bring a lover home, as will placing shoes on the floor so that the toe of one will touch the middle of the other and then reciting, "When I my true love want to see, I put my shoes in the shape of a T."

Missouri Ozarks Legends & Lore

Death

An unusual clicking or rumbling in a clock is an omen that a relative or close friend is dying that very moment. If a clock that has not run for a long time suddenly begins to strike, there will be a death in the house. The number of chimes indicates the number of days or weeks or months until it happens.

There's a difference of opinion about this interpretation.

In my own experience, I encountered something like this when my mother was in an end-of-life hospice with just days to live. A clock in her condo that had not been working for quite some time began ticking and the pendulum moved side to side on its own accord.

Other folklore omens include hearing any unusual household noise, like the sound of cloth tearing, as a death sign. Many Ozark folk claim to hear death bones shortly before someone dies. Raps, ticks, knocks or bells are omens of death, as is a sharp snapping noise heard in a log cabin—said to be caused by a beetle with a singular gift of divination.

Death bell omens manifest in several ways. Church bells ringing on their own accord signify natural disaster, such as flood or fire. Ringing in the ears signifies that a death will occur, as does a tinkling sound. A loud bell ringing signifies the death of a prominent person.

Fish

Ozark fishermen know that an east wind is the worst possible bad omen. Bass won't bite when there is lightning. If a dragonfly lands on a fisherman's bobber, there will be bad luck. Fish bite best in the dark of the moon.

Household Superstitions

It's bad luck to drop a dishrag, and many woman throw salt over their shoulders to drop the curse. If a woman drops a dishrag, she knows that a dirty visitor is on the way. If the cloth falls in a tight wad, the visitor is a woman. If the cloth spreads out on the floor, a man is expected. If the cloth is dropped twice, expect a hungry visitor. Dropping a fork signifies that a man is coming, but a case knife indicates that a woman is coming.

If a rocking chair moves along the floor when someone is rocking, expect company before nightfall and prepare for guests.

49

An itching right eye is an omen for good luck, but a left eye itching is an omen of disappointment. This, unless you believe, as some do, that an itching right eye is an omen of bad luck, while the left signifies that good news is a-comin'.

Mountain Medicine

Old sores, cancers and lesions are sometimes treated with powdered bones of a person long dead. One source of bones for hill people is Indian graves and Bluff Dweller burials under cave ledges dating back more than ten thousand years. Bones are broken into small pieces with a hammer and then ground to powder to use as medicine.

Mountain medicine adopts the belief that physiological phenomena are in line with the waxing and waning of the moon. Yarb, meaning healing plant medicines, are taken in the dark of the waning moon. Signs of the zodiac are considered, such as stomach trouble being aggravated when the moon is in Cancer, throat problem during the sign of Taurus, venereal infections in Scorpio and so on. Many old hillfolk wouldn't have surgery unless the appropriate sign is indicated on the calendar. Hillfolk believe that unpleasant-tasting medicine is most efficient. The worse it tastes, the better it works.

Pregnancy and Childbirth

Some believe that if a pregnant woman crosses a running stream, she will die. A pregnant woman who "puts up" fruit will spoil the fruit. The sex of a child can be predetermined—for a boy, place a knife under the mattress and for a girl, a skillet.

Trees

Many old people believe that ironwood trees are planted by the devil's agents. Sassafras trees sprout from grubworms, and others believe that mistletoe (or witch's broom) sprouts spontaneously from bird droppings. The pawpaw tree is known to be connected to witchcraft.

Water Witch

The sinister-sounding term *water witch* labels a waterfinder who has no association with the devil—also, the practice of water witching has nothing whatsoever to do with witchcraft, but rather describes a person who searches for underground water by using a dowsing rod.

Weather Signs

Randolph's *Ozark Magic and Folklore* states that a rainbow in the evening means clear weather, but a rainbow in the morning means there will be a storm within twenty-four hours.

Weather is predictable by omens and signs, depending on the hill or hollow, but no matter where you are when you see a tornado coming, run into a field and stick a knife into the ground with the edge of the blade facing toward the approaching funnel. The blade will split the wind and protect you from the funnel.

A tornado or severe storm is imminent if you see a hog looking at the sky when there is nothing there to attract its attention. When a hog carries wood in its mouth, a storm is coming.

A ring around the moon is a sign of bad weather. A blue line on the horizon at sunset predicts rain the next day.

A red sunset means twenty-four hours of dry weather. Lightning in a southern sky means dry weather, but seen in any other direction indicates rain. If the leaves of a tree show their underside in a breeze, expect rain within a few hours. The size of the first raindrops indicate what kind of rain will follow. Small raindrops indicate rainy weather. Large raindrops indicate a brief shower.

Witch Ball

In the Ozark Mountains, a witch ball is made from black hair that is rolled with beeswax into a hard round pellet about the size of a marble and is used in curses. In Ozark folklore, a witch who wants to kill someone throws the ball at the intended victim. When someone in the Ozarks is killed by a witch's curse, a witch ball is found near the body.

Missouri Ozarks Legends & Lore

Yarb and Power Doctors

Yarb and Power doctors in Ozark folklore are backwoods healers, yet each has a completely different approach to the art of healing. Yarb doctors use plant medicines, whereas Power doctors use charms, spells, prayers, amulets, exorcisms and a variety of magic.

Bell Francis (1895–1918), my maternal great-grandmother, was a Madison County farmer's daughter who was gifted in Yarb healing, according to George Knott, Francis family historian, who heard it from Bell's own brother, who labeled Bell as a witch. What gives this label credence is that when Bell died in 1918, likely from the Spanish flu pandemic, a feather death crown was found in her feather pillow. But it was not an ordinary death crown—it had a witches ladder coiled into its center.

Bell Francis (1895–1918), backwoods healer. *Author's collection.*

Death crown folklore comes from Irish Appalachian tradition, which was brought to the Ozarks when the Scotch-Irish settled here during the early 1800s. Death crowns are a good omen, as the crown magically forms in the pillow when a spirit leaves the body and signifies that a good person went straight to heaven.

Witches ladder folklore indicates that a ladder is almost always made of teal wool yarn, as was Bell's ladder. The yarn is pierced, by design, at one-inch intervals with small feathers that would have been used to keep track of spells and chants. Witches ladders can be used for healing, or they can be used for spells, according to folklore. My hunch is that Bell put the ladder in her pillow when she came down with the Spanish flu after delivering a set of twin girls in January 1918. This is the condensed version of Bell's mysterious story of many layers.

And now for the flip side of Yarb healers! Power healers depend entirely on charms, spells, prayers, amulets, exorcisms and a variety of magic. Power doctors, or backwoods specialists, claim to be endowed with supernatural power to cure specific ailments. Power doctors are usually old women and can cool fevers simply by laying on hands; they can draw the heat out of a burn using spells with words that aren't in the Bible.

52

Missouri Ozarks Legends & Lore

There is a dilemma here shrouded in ambiguity. Because Bell was a farmer's daughter, it's logical to imagine her as a Yarb healer. But does the witches ladder indicate a Power ritual? And does it matter that Bell was a caulbearer, meaning she was born with a mystical veil over her face—an omen of someone gifted with extraordinary ability?

Chapter 6

OZARK GHOST STORIES

> *Then away out in the woods I heard that kind of a sound that a ghost makes when it wants to tell about something that's on its mind and can't make itself understood, and so can't rest easy in its grave, and has to go about that way every night grieving.*
> —*Mark Twain*

Even those who don't believe in ghosts are afraid of them. The best ghost stories are born of decay, lonesome places, deserted buildings and covered bridges—same as ghost stories told everywhere. Here are a few from the Missouri Ozarks guaranteed to raise hackles.

BLACK DOG OMEN

In folklore, the black dog is a nocturnal apparition said to be associated with the devil, or it is described as a ghost or supernatural hellhound. It can be a shapeshifter and is considered to be an omen of death.

However, the notion of guardian black dogs appeared around 1900 in Europe; these do not typically appear in Ozark stories. This folklore speaks to the rare guardian black dogs that are not omens of death but rather guides for lost travelers and protectors from danger. Another version of the guardian black dog is as a protector of children.

When an Ozark fiddler named Jake Lakey was killed at a dance around 1900, two young boys were sent several miles on horseback to break the

MISSOURI OZARKS LEGENDS & LORE

news to his wife. When they told her that a large black dog ran beside their horses all the way, Mrs. Lakey knew that Jake was dead.

Disembodied Footsteps

In McDonald County, Missouri, an elderly lady sat alone in her two-room cabin. The door was bolted and windows locked when she heard the door latch move. Heavy footsteps moved across the floor, with boots squeaking at every step. She then heard the dipper rattle in the water bucket. She ran into the kitchen, but nobody was there. The door was still bolted, and the windows were still locked.

Disembodied Voices

A Taney County farmer sought help from a local lawyer, claiming that he could hear his dead daughter singing out in the woods every afternoon. She had been dead several months, so when the skeptics also heard her singing, they were bewildered. The female voice gradually got louder, and the words were clear. They rushed toward the source of the sound but did not see the singer. The lawyer did not believe in ghosts, but he admitted to hearing the singing and claimed that he didn't know what it was.

In another story, a savage, ill-tempered woman passed away suddenly. She had always fought with her husband, and although he was suspected to have murdered her, no proof was found. After her death, the widower remained in the same cabin. Neighbors continued to hear fighting, dishes shattering, shouting and cursing and furniture being thrown around. They went to give it the once-over and found the man sitting in front of the fire, quiet as a mouse. The noise was coming from the lean-to kitchen, where, clear as day, the woman's voice carried on with familiar cursing and obscene phrases. The widower advised the neighbors to remain calm because she wasn't mad at nobody but him.

Ephemeral Sightings

At the old game park near Mincy, Missouri, a woman clearly saw a small cabin in the not too far distance. She'd never seen a cabin there before, so

55

Missouri Ozarks Legends & Lore

she got out her field glasses and noticed smoke coming out of the chimney. Next day, the cabin was gone.

In Madison County, Missouri, a group of local people traveling along Highway 61 sometime in 1932 noticed the charred remains of a house that had burned down to the ground. Only the chimney, cookstove and two iron beds were left standing in the ashes. Upon returning to the house a few days later, they were astounded to see it intact, and people who lived nearby claimed that there had been no fire.

Hauntings and Money

The lack of money is the root of all evil.
—*Mark Twain*

In Stone County, Missouri, Beadtray Mountain is notorious for its many ghost stories. The mountain is a landmark of strange incidents, its reputation unparalleled. Hillfolk simply avoid it altogether. Legend has it that Spaniards buried a treasure-trove of gold on the mountain just before they were all killed by Indians. At night, sobs and groans are heard on the mountain by credible people who claim that the story is not based on hearsay.

Many a rumor is connected to buried or lost money. Lucid dreams or ghostly visits do not lead to finding treasure; however, Wayne County, Missouri, is the exception. Near the town of Taskee, an old man was murdered in a farmhouse. His ghost appeared there at intervals, but nobody would live in the house after his murder. Then, a traveler who had no fear of ghosts stayed there. He built a fire in the hearth and later woke to see the ghost of the old man. The ghost pleaded with him, saying that he could not be at rest until somebody found the money and used it for something useful. The ghost led the traveler outdoors and then removed some bricks from the chimney and pulled a large sum of money out of hiding. The ghost was never seen again after that.

Headless Apparition

In Braggadocio, Dunklin County, Missouri, a headless dog lives in a hollow elm tree outside of town and runs through the village streets on moonlit nights.

Humorous Ghost Stories

For entertainment, pioneer hillmen would gather with others to socialize, and sometimes that included swapping supernatural tales. Often the ghost stories they shared would be tongue-in-cheek humorous about their belief in ghosts. For example, there was a superstitious fellow who was always afraid to walk past the graveyard after dark. His friends would reassure him that ghosts are not known to hurt people. To that he replied, "Maybe not, but I don't want 'em a-follerin' me around!"

Or this one: Old lady Jones and her two ne'er-do-well sons were stealing Jim Bray's sheep. The old woman would wait in the graveyard while her sons went into Bray's field and got one of the herd. If the animal were not fat enough, she'd make the boys go back and get a better sheep.

Meanwhile, disabled Jim Bray was a-wishing he could get to the graveyard, lie in wait for the thieves an' stay that 'til he did ketch 'em. An so his boys picked up their old man and carried him across the pasture to the graveyard. Old lady Jones barely saw their shadows a-comin' in the dark night an' thought it was her boys returning with the sheep. "'Bout time you-uns was a-comin'," she crocked hoarsely. "Is he fat?" she said and pinched the old man's leg.

With wild yells of terror, the Bray boys dropped their pappy and tuck out for home, but the old man was at their heels when they reached the cabin. Jim Bray would boast the rest of his life that the Old Boy riz up out of hell and cured his rheumatism, after the doctors had plum give up.

A young man had been visiting his sweetheart, and as he rode away on horseback, she called out that she'd be with him all the way home. Soon he noticed something ethereal floating and trailing behind him. This frightened him, and so he put spurs to his horse. But the white floating shape followed him just as close. Terrified, he raced home, even losing his hat in his haste to flee. He was certain that his sweetheart had bewitched him and would have nothing to do with her. Months later, he found the hat in the briar patch, with a remnant of gauze tucked under the snakeskin band. It was too late—the girl had already married someone else and moved to Oklahoma.

One last humorous ghostly tale involves two men transporting a corpse with a horse-drawn wagon. The deceased was tightly wrapped in canvas and

Missouri Ozarks Legends & Lore

placed under straw in the back of the wagon. When the two men stopped at a roadside tavern for whiskey, a drunken country boy climbed under the hay and went to sleep. The two men returned and continued their journey, drinking more whiskey and getting rowdy. One called out to the corpse to get up and have a sniffer with them. The groggy drunk sat up and said he didn't mind if he did.

Justice

In Pineville, Missouri, a deceased mother intervened on behalf of her children, who were being mistreated by a cruel stepmother. One day, the stepmother was sitting alone in her cabin when a violent blow put her flat on the floor, and a loud voice cried out, "Be good to my children!"

Chapter 7

OZARK MONSTER FOLKLORE

When in doubt, tell the truth.
—*Mark Twain*

Momo, the Missouri Monster (Pike County)

Momo, a pet name for the Missouri Monster, refers to the legendary Missouri creature often compared to Bigfoot or Sasquatch. Missourians first got word of Momo on the mid-afternoon of July 11, 1972, when reports of sightings poured into the Louisiana, Missouri police department. In the small Missouri town located on the western banks of the Mississippi River, numerous residents reported seeing a seven-foot-tall creature.

Of the many Louisiana residents who claim to have seen Momo, all described the creature as having a disgusting smell paired with long, shaggy fur that concealed its face. And it had a low, menacing growl. Some reported fleeting glimpses of something in the woods, while others smelled something beastly. Some heard haunting cries and inhuman screams. In a nutshell, many reports described a monster that walked upright, had black fur that covered its entire body and sported a large, furry, pumpkin-size head and red glowing eyes.

The sightings soon gave birth to frenzy, as some residents reported coming face to face with Momo, while others reported having their cars overturned by the beast. Two women hid in their car, watching Momo eat their peanut butter sandwich and then run off into the woods. Most disturbingly, three

Missouri Ozarks Legends & Lore

young siblings (Terry, Wiley and Doris Harrison) saw the creature in their backyard near Marzolf Hill, bloody and carrying a dead dog. Richard Alan Murry, a lifelong local and the former town fire chief, reported seeing something move in the woods as he drove alongside a creek that runs through town. When his headlights illuminated the upright creature, it disappeared into thick woods. The credentialed skeptic was astounded to witness something beyond a doubt that he had formerly judged to be nonsense.

Within a short time, others caught glimpses of Momo as it allegedly stalked Missouri's wooded hills accompanied by disembodied voices, mysterious lights and unexplained objects streaking across the sky. After a rash of early sightings, the encounters fizzled and then stopped altogether.

The Momo episode sparked debates that continue into 2021 via podcasts that speculate on the origin of the beast. Assuming it actually arrived out of nowhere and then stayed a short period of time before disappearing, one can see four viable options: hysteria, hoax, UFO or a multi-dimensional slip. The consensus is that the sightings were not totally hysteria-based. Credible people witnessed them, and the descriptions of Momo were consistent. If Momo were a hoax, there would have been a motive, such as to create a tourist destination. Except for the outstanding Momoburger offered at the local Dairy Queen, that didn't happen. The UFO theory with an alien Momo creature gets ruled out because, well, why would Momo come to this planet just to stink it up and then leave? Also, it's unlikely that a creature sophisticated enough for space travel would go around eating family pets. That leaves the option that Momo was from another dimension. Like Bigfoot, Momo's appearance best fits the notion that it slipped into our dimension without an agenda and then returned to its own dimension likely as bewildered as our Missouri townspeople. Nothing gained, nothing lost.

Footprints said to belong to Momo have been studied by two experts, with one claiming that they are a hoax and the other, Lawrence Curtis, director of the Oklahoma City Zoo, identifying it as the print of an unknown primate species.

The town of Louisiana sits between St. Louis and Hannibal, all river towns. Specifically, it's seventy miles north of St. Louis and about thirty miles south of Hannibal. Imagine Hannibal native Mark Twain, who both arrived at and departed this planet during the presence of Halley's Comet, crafting a story around Momo set in the Mississippi Valley.

Check out the 2019 horror film documentary titled *Momo: The Missouri Monster*, or the 2019 book titled *Momo: The Strange Case of the Missouri Monster*.

Momo: The Missouri Monster

This movie traces what happened in the small river town of Louisiana, Missouri, back in 1972, when Momo the Missouri Monster showed up one day amid multiple UFO sightings.

I recommend watching this campy docu-horror film. To its credit, it provides very good-quality visual imagery of the bucolic town by way of aerial photography and offers private interviews with townspeople who experienced the phenomenon of Momo firsthand. This, along with information gained through a pop horror radio show, sets the stage for the story of a town that was turned upside down in an instant.

The hilly landscape of small-town Louisiana is located on the western bank of the Mississippi River, where river and railroad trade have sustained the tobacco farming town for well over one hundred years. Marzolf Hill, also known as Star Hill, is a town landmark that eerily resembles an Indian burial mound. The hill is dubbed "The Playground" because it is the perfect landscape for childhood adventure, complete with a natural cave and a dilapidated abandoned house.

The documentary moves on to profile Louisiana (founded 1860) one year before Momo was frequently sighted, and it registers Louisiana as a place where unusual things happened before Momo showed up, where frequent sightings of ghosts and enormous birds and monsters inspire local folklore.

The film opens with two incompatible teenage girls (Mills and Ryan) driving a red-orange VW Bug along a Missouri backroad while headed to an Alice Cooper concert, circa 1971. They're arguing about chicken heads and the Carpenters' serene music verses Alice Cooper's edgy genre. When they stop along the river for a picnic lunch, their sense of smell is assaulted by the stench of Momo. When the girls spot Momo, hysteria ensues, and Momo chases them straight into the safety of the Bug. In the commotion, car keys are left behind, and the girls are seemingly trapped in the small car. As fate would have it, Momo is scared away by the blast of their car horn, allowing one of the girls to run back to the picnic area and retrieve the key, only to start the engine and find themselves stuck in the mud.

The documentary then moves to one year later and features local restaurant owner, Edgar Harrison, whose three children were the first to experience Momo in 1972. The Harrisons lived at the base of Marzolf Hill, with the back of their house oriented to the hill. His two boys and their elder sister were home alone when Momo appeared from the woods, carrying a dead animal and growling at them. Later, Edgar explored the area after dark, only to find enormous animal tracks and the sound of disembodied voices.

Edgar was a religious man, so you can imagine his disbelief sometime later when flashes of light and bright orbs flew from Marzolf Hill and hovered over his house during a backyard prayer meeting.

Soon a wave of UFO sightings had people convinced that Momo was an extraterrestrial. As more strange activities caused panic, mob mentality took over, and soon the small river town was monster central to hundreds of monster hunters brave enough to follow Momo's mournful howl and three-toed tracks. With so many huntsmen likely to shoot at anything that moved, it became dangerous to search the woods, and the pressure to kill Momo intensified.

During one hunting expedition, a group discovered a lean-to nest in the woods—Momo's lair, constructed of branches and debris. Fear stricken at the sight of it, Edgar ran into the woods, as any crazed alpha male eager to shoot a monster would do. Sooner than later, he fell into a pit near the lair that contained human bones scattered about. When Momo appeared above the pit's edge and peered down at his prey, Edgar aimed his shotgun and shot the beast between the eyes. The monster mysteriously fizzled and vanished. Meanwhile, other hunters in the woods saw strange lights and heard disembodied voices that emanated from all directions.

The Momo phenomenon eventually faded away, leaving a town changed forever.

Ozark Howler

The Ozark Howler is another legendary creature that trolls the remote areas of southern Missouri and northwest Arkansas, and it has also been spotted as far west as Oklahoma and as far south as Texas. Its ominous cry is like the melding of a wolf's howl and elk's bugle. The melding is likely a mating call to which female howlers are drawn, following it without hesitation into the dense Ozark wilderness in the hopes of making little baby howlers, which I'd wager are adorable.

The Ozark Howler is typically described as a bear-sized, cat-like creature, its thick body supported by stocky legs. Black shaggy hair covers its body, and some witnesses enhance its monster savoir faire by adding horns. At any rate, the Ozark Howler's glowing red eyes eerily reflect light, even when there is no obvious source.

MISSOURI OZARKS LEGENDS & LORE

Anthropologists speculate that the creature might be a misidentified large cat. Historians speculate that the creature might be a cultural variant of the Dark Dogs of Death legend found in European folklore that was brought to the Ozarks by the Scotch-Irish settlers. There is no mention of parallel dimensions or UFOs accompanied by extraterrestrials, and there's not even a hint of disembodied voices. Yet the theory does not deny the howler's existence. Cryptozoologists take a skeptical view of the howler, referring to it as an animal that people claim to see but whose existence has not been confirmed.

Whether the Ozark Howler is real or not, it has been used as a fictional character in numerous novels, including the Mason Dixon children's book series by Eric R. Ashe; *Billy Bob's Howler*, by Ross Malone; and *Hunt the Ozark Howler*, by Jan Fields. A comic book called *Tale of an Ozark Howler* by Kelly Reno was published in 2008 and features the creature as its main character. In 1973, the magazine *Cryptic Universe* published a science-fiction short story about the Ozark Howler titled "The Hair of the Black Howler." Likewise, the Ozark Howler has been inspiration for poets and songwriters and is well documented in the Encyclopedia of Arkansas.

And so, by now, you must be intrigued by the Missouri Ozarks as an enchanting, yet unsung, mountain destination. No doubt you've felt its mystical vibe and labeled yourself as the creative type drawn there to get grounded. Welcome! You're in good company.

Chapter 8

HAUNTS AND CURIOSITIES OF THE SALEM PLATEAU

I did not attend his funeral, but I sent a nice letter saying I approved of it.
—*Mark Twain*

Missouri Ozark mountain towns never lack for ghostly legends and lore, what with bobbing orbs and glowing gravestones, phantom music and spirits roaming century-old buildings. If this is your cup of tea, consider the following well-documented places when planning your haunted Ozark travels.

BOON COUNTY: COLUMBIA, THOMAS JEFFERSON'S TOMBSTONE, UMC

Even though Thomas Jefferson had specific instructions for his obelisk gravestone, he didn't specify where the tombstone would be located. But perhaps he should have, as it resides on the campus of the University of Missouri–Columbia. That's about in the middle of the state, in rural Missouri halfway between St. Louis and Kansas City.

Jefferson stipulated the medium as coarse stone inscribed with his proudest accomplishments, such as author of the Declaration of American Independence and the Virginia Statute for Religious Freedom and father of the University of Virginia (but notably omitting serving as president of the United States).

Missouri Ozarks Legends & Lore

The grave marker and accompanying marble epitaph were originally erected at Monticello, seven years after Jefferson's death in 1826. In 1883, Jefferson's descendants donated the tombstone to the university at Columbia, Missouri. To this day, the reason for the choice is not entirely clear, but it's not entirely arbitrary either. Perhaps it is linked to the fact that the Missouri university was the first founded within the territory that was acquired in the Louisiana Purchase during Jefferson's tenure as president. Or perhaps it's because the school's design inspired Jefferson's plans for the University of Virginia, of which he was so proud.

No matter how or why the obelisk landed in Missouri, the tombstone can be found in front of the Residence on Francis Quadrangle, while the marble epitaph is on display at Jesse Hall. A replica of the obelisk was erected at Jefferson's grave at Monticello.

Cape Girardeau County: Haunted Glenn House Cape Girardeau

325 South Spanish Street, Cape Girardeau, MO 63703

Glenn House, built in 1883, is haunted by a Christmas ghost. The mansion was built by Edwin Dean for his daughter, Lulu, and her husband, David Glenn. But when banker Glenn lost much of his fortune in 1915, they moved out. The property fell into disrepair and is now a house museum listed in the National Register of Historic Places.

The Glenn House is a window into Victorian-era life, but with paranormal undertones. The board president of the Historical Association of Greater Cape Girardeau reached out to the *Ghost Hunters* crew when volunteers were driven away by sounds of children laughing, footsteps and cool breezes on the staircase in an otherwise empty house. During the holiday season, volunteers found gifts that had been unwrapped during the night when nobody was in the house.

They decided that it was time for someone to take an objective look at the phenomenon. The *Ghost Hunters* crew spent a week investigating the Glenn House during the fall of 2019. The crew debunked some of the unexplained happenings, but others had no logical answer. The house was featured on a *Ghost Hunters* episode that aired in May 2020.

65

Missouri Ozarks Legends & Lore

Cape Girardeau County:
Haunted Lorimier Cemetery

500 North Fountain Street, Cape Girardeau, MO, 63701

Listed in the National Register of Historic Places, this haunted Mississippi river town cemetery, circa early 1800s, is home to a phenomenon known as the Tapping Ghost. It manifests as a sensation that feels like something tapping your shoulder—like a nut falling from a tree and hitting your shoulder. Countless people have felt the tapping, only to find nobody there, even when they're alone in the cemetery. Many have witnessed ghosts wandering the cemetery in the evening.

Cape Girardeau's old cemetery boasts a long, storied history that begins in the early 1800s and spans religion, race, Civil War and smallpox. It is the location of several mass burials. Of the six thousand who came to rest here, more than one thousand were Civil War soldiers killed by smallpox. Others in mass graves were victims of steamboat accidents. Many graves are unmarked, and records for the cemetery burned in a courthouse fire. Nobody knows for sure how many people are buried on the hallowed grounds.

Lorimier Cemetery, listed in the National Register of Historic Places, is home to a phenomenon known as the Tapping Ghost. *Courtesy of Wikimedia Commons, Larry J. Summary.*

Missouri Ozarks Legends & Lore

Cape Girardeau County: Haunted Port Cape Girardeau Restaurant and Lounge

19 North Water Street, Cape Girardeau, MO 63701

Port Cape Girardeau Restaurant and Lounge in Warehouse Row, housed in a circa 1860 warehouse, is haunted by a female ghost nicknamed "Belle." The bartender who named her said that soon after he decided on the name, a bell in the downstairs hall began ringing on its own accord, as if to affirm the name he chose. The apparition was seen dressed in nineteenth-century attire, and customers have reported inexplicable noises and have heard footsteps. Orbs are seen in the bar and show up in photographs.

Cape Girardeau County: Southeast Missouri State University

One University Plaza, Cape Girardeau, MO 63701

Southeast Missouri State University's Cheney Hall is rumored to be haunted by a female student who committed suicide there in a bathtub. Folks say that the door slams by itself, and unexplained noises are heard in the room. The Music Building is also said to be haunted by apparitions.

Cape Girardeau County: UFO Crash 1941 Cape Girardeau

When responders came to investigate what first appeared to be a plane crash just outside the city of Cape Girardeau, their lives were changed forever. Medics, a minister who'd been brought along to read last rites to crash victims, reporters, police and some military personnel who witnessed the craft and dead alien bodies were sworn to secrecy that night. However, some retained photographs or artifacts and, decades later, made deathbed confessions to their offspring regarding the crash that predates Roswell, New Mexico, by six years.

Missouri Ozarks Legends & Lore

Douglas County: Angel of Ava

Back in 1940, it appears that the folks of the small Ozark town named Ava were visited by what would become the legend of the Angel of Ava. When envelopes of money began arriving in mailboxes of local hillfolk, the expression "Angel of Ava" surfaced. The divine amount of money varied but was about $100 per person—or more than $1,800 in 2021 currency.

Iron County: Arcadia Academy

Now listed in the National Register of Historic Places, Arcadia Academy was originally built as a Methodist high school in 1840 and was later used as a Civil War hospital for Union troops. After that, it was a girls' Catholic school until it became a bed-and-breakfast and an antique store.

The nuns who used to run the school are buried at a cemetery on the grounds; they are said to haunt the place. As documented by the organization Haunted Places, photographs taken here show orbs, vortexes and strange mists. If interested, check out photographs on the website and look for wavy lines suspended in the image, foggy mists or round balls of light.

Iron County: Haunted Ironton Parlor Bed-and-Breakfast

This beautiful turreted 1908 house was briefly a funeral home during the 1960s and is now an inn rumored to be home to many spirits. They ring the doorbells at all hours, turn clocks and radios on and off and activate other electrical objects. They might even speak to you or touch you.

Jefferson County, Dittmer: Haunted Morse Mill Hotel

8850 Old Morse Mill Spur, Hillsboro, MO 63050

Built in 1816 as a farmhouse, the Morse Mill Hotel had its heyday in the 1920s and 1930s. Clara Bow, Charles Lindbergh, Jesse James and Al Capone are among the famous guests who have stayed here, as well as the serial

68

MISSOURI OZARKS LEGENDS & LORE

Morse Mill Hotel haunts are well documented. It has been visited by Charles Lindbergh, Jesse James and Al Capone, as well as the serial killer Bertha Gifford, who killed her victims by arsenic poisoning. *Courtesy of Angelia Wiley.*

killer Bertha Gifford, who killed her victims by poisoning them with arsenic. Haunts are well documented with audio and visual accounts. As stated on the Morse Mill Hotel website, visitors who don't engage or confront the paranormal presence don't encounter the activity, nor do they see or hear anything unusual.

It was settled in 1816 as a farmhouse when Missouri was still a Spanish territory within the Louisiana Territory. In 1856, John H. Morse, a bridge builder and Confederate sympathizer, purchased and then expanded the building using building materials meant to last forever: limestone twenty-four inches thick as foundation walls and three-by-five-inch hardwood flooring. Likewise, by way of the original wood floors, you will be stepping where Jesse James, Al Capone, Charlie Chaplin and Charles Lindbergh have walked.

A tunnel runs under the house to nearby Big River and is thought to have been a part of the Session Railroad, or Chip Trail, which had the reverse function of the Underground Railroad.

69

Missouri Ozarks Legends & Lore

Check out morsemillhotel.com or theozarktraveler.com for more of its history, eyewitness accounts of ghostly encounters and pictures of anomalies, or you can make tour/lodging reservations.

Jefferson County, Valles Mines: Haunted Lost History Museum

This 1749 house museum is haunted, and travelers driving past claim to have seen the apparition of a soldier staring down onto the street. Other activity reported here includes people being touched by unseen hands and strange anomalies showing up in photographs.

Ripley County: Doniphan, Haunted Oak Ridge Cemetery

Oak Ridge Cemetery in Doniphan has a female apparition that is often seen among the graves, and disembodied voices are heard as well. A local legend has it that the statue of Belle Neal comes to life at midnight.

Ste. Genevieve County: Ste. Genevieve, Haunted Jacques Guibourd Historic House

Jacques Guibourd Historic House (aka La Maison de Guibourd or Guibourd Valle House) is an example of *poteaux-sur-solle* (post in soil) sealed with bouzillage (a mix of clay and grass used as fill) construction. The structure was built around 1806 and was the home of Jacques Jean Rene Guibourd and his family.

Not only does the harpsicord play on its own accord, but visitors have observed apparitions and heard footsteps in the servants' quarters and have been awakened by banging, breaking glass, furniture being thrown and other sounds.

Missouri Ozarks Legends & Lore

Ste. Genevieve County: Ste. Genevieve, Haunted Main Street Inn Bed-and-Breakfast

The Main Street Inn Bed-and-Breakfast is a three-story red brick building, circa 1882, with a Mansard roof. Rumor is that a man who died here in the 1890s haunts it. He makes a lot of noise up on the top floor in the early morning hours, but he is completely harmless.

St. Louis City: Alexian Brothers Hospital Exorcism

If the 1949 St. Louis account of an exorcism of a young boy at Alexian Brothers Hospital is true, then the truth really is stranger than fiction; the real-life events that inspired *The Exorcist* are tied to the history of St. Louis University in St. Louis, Missouri.

When a young boy tried to contact his aunt's spirit using a Ouija board, strange things began happening to him. After a medical doctor, psychologist and minister were unable to help the boy, the family went to St. Louis for help from relatives, but bizarre happenings followed them to Missouri. St. Louis Jesuits stepped in to aid the family, first at the St. Louis University campus and then at the Alexian Brothers Hospital, where the struggle ended on Easter Monday 1949, according to Saint Louis University's website (www.slu.edu).

St. Louis City: Quirky City Museum

North Sixteenth Street, St. Louis, MO 63103

City Museum has been named one of the great public spaces by the Project for Public Spaces and has won other local and international awards as a must-see destination. It is known as a wild, singular vision of the oddball artistic mind of Bob Cassilly.

But Bob didn't work alone. He and his former wife, Gail Soliwoda, collaborated on much of its creation. Gail Soliwoda Cassilly's autobiography, *Saltwater*, features her involvement with the museum with the aforementioned artistic visionary and tells her life story leading up to the creation of City Museum. As a memoir author and enthusiast, I rate *Saltwater*

71

Missouri Ozarks Legends & Lore

City Museum has been described as a wild, singular vision of an oddball artistic mind. It's been named one of the great public spaces by the Project for Public Spaces, designating it as a must-see destination. *Courtesy of Wikimedia Commons, Chris857.*

as the most intriguing memoir I've ever come across, and it changed me for the reading of it. This visual artist, acclaimed in her own right, approaches her matchless story with humor and dignity.

City Museum has been described as a museum of the city of St. Louis, as well as a children's museum where the children are part of the scenery. Likewise, it is a place where adults release their inner child for the time of their lives. Housed in 600,000 square feet of the former International Shoe building near downtown, the museum has given new life to an area that was in hopeless decline. Once abandoned and derelict, the now trendy district is home to art galleries and restaurants, as well as upscale loft homes in historic commercial buildings.

The museum's mission is to preserve the city's architectural artifacts that were being discarded with tear-downs. Not to be missed is the jet airplane shell mounted five stories above the ground, easily accessible by crawling through an open air cage (also suspended five stories in open air). This, and the rooftop school bus suspended half way off the roof, perfectly complement the rooftop Ferris wheel with sweeping views of downtown.

MISSOURI OZARKS LEGENDS & LORE

Sometimes repurposed and other times used in their original form, the pieces of City Museum are pieces of the city of St. Louis, assembled from an ever-expanding collection of reclaimed architectural relics. For example, there's the former chute that conveyed finished pairs of shoes from the top floor to the ground floor, repurposed as a ten-story spiral slide. Starting at the roof, it takes you all the way down to the entrance of the enchanted cave.

City Museum must be experienced in three dimensions to truly comprehend its genius—you have to see it to believe it. Check out more information at Atlas Obscura (https://www.atlasobscura.com/places/city-museum) before your visit.

St. Louis County: Wildwood, Haunted Zombie Road

A short drive westbound on old Route 66 into St. Louis County brings you to the city of Wildwood and its haunted Zombie Road, an ancient path that was upgraded to a dirt and gravel road in the 1860s to provide access to the Meramec River and railroad tracks that run parallel to it.

Not only is Zombie Road known as Missouri's most haunted, but it's also considered to be one of the most haunted roads in the world. Now, that's a reputation to be reckoned with, especially considering that during daylight hours the two-mile stretch is used for recreation. The ten-foot-wide hike and bike path meanders through scenic Ozark landscape before ending near the Meramec River in Glencoe. During daylight hours, it is known as Lawler Ford Road or the Al Foster Trail, but after darkness falls, it is exclusively the infamous Zombie Road.

The image shown in this section of the bright orb crossing Zombie Road at night is used courtesy of the Paranormal Task Force. The image was captured by the late Tom Halstead, photographer for the organization. However, Greg Meyers, president of Paranormal Task Force, told me that the night they investigated Zombie, they saw visual orbs of various sizes and different speeds—without the aid of a camera. Now, that's not typical. Most of the time they show up in photographs but are not seen by the naked eye.

Any good ghost story has earthly elements that support paranormal activity, and Zombie Road is no exception. In fact, Zombie is the poster child for a setting sure to be haunted. Moving water, the presence of iron and limestone containing quartz crystal run amok along Zombie's wooded Ozark landscape, along with its rich history as fodder for the haints. Not only

73

MISSOURI OZARKS LEGENDS & LORE

Zombie Road runs alongside the Meramec River in the city of Wildwood and is alleged to be one of the most haunted roads in the world. Pictured is a moving orb on that was dubbed Super Orb by the Paranormal Task Force team during an investigation. *Courtesy of Paranormal Task Force, Tom Halstead, photographer.*

does Zombie carry the perfect setting with paranormal earth elements and an intriguing history, but it also sits within the 37th parallel band known as the "Paranormal Highway."

As early as 1950, Zombie Road had gained its reputation as a place where strange things happen. The name comes from the lore of an escaped mental patient who hid out in the woods. According to legend, all that was ever found of the escapee, who went by the nickname "Zombie," were his discarded bloody ragged clothes, according to a St. Louis Underground YouTube interview featuring the phenomena of Zombie Road.

Legendary stories of hauntings tell of spectral images, shadowy figures and other nonhuman entities peering out from the woods. Local lore has it that the trail is watched over by shadow people, as witnessed by many after dark trolling for a good scare. It has a long history of use, from Native Americans to early settlers and from Confederate Rebels marching off to war to Union soldiers moving along the path. Spectral Indians, soldiers and clusters of ghost children are seen watching from the cover of trees in the

74

Missouri Ozarks Legends & Lore

densely wooded landscape. The tortured souls of men killed in industrial accidents make their presence known on Zombie Road. Documented deaths are also associated with Zombie Road. The Meramec riverbank is known for its drownings. On this ancient Osage path to the river, railroad workers have died, and people have been hit by trains.

This center of paranormal activity is a hub for Satanic rituals and séances, as well as for teenagers who come down to party. In the 1950s, a group of Ladue High School kids were partying in the woods when one guy fell off a bluff to his death. In the unlikely event you need to identify marauders by category, it goes like this: high school kids have beer, Satanists use a flaming ring of fire and mediums levitate.

If you can muster the moxie to navigate the haunted path after dark, be aware that the Ozark haints of Zombie Road watch from the trees, awaiting an encounter with curiosity-seekers who navigate the secluded path after dark. But haints aren't the only ones watching. Just ask the St. Louis Underground team, whose members acquired citations for trespassing on the trail after hours.

Zombie Road is located in the city of Wildwood, west of St. Louis, Missouri, near the intersection of State Highway 109 and Old State Road. It's open one half hour before sunrise and closed one half hour after sunset.

SHANNON COUNTY:
EMINENCE, ECHO BLUFF STATE PARK

The lodge in Echo Bluff State Park is rated as a three-star lodge, and it's located in the Ozarks Mark Twain Forest. Known as the "Gateway to the Ozarks," the park is open year-round.

WASHINGTON COUNTY: CALEDONIA,
HAUNTED RUGGLES-EVANS-DENT HOUSE

116 South Missouri 21, Caledonia, MO 63631

Built in 1849 by Jacob Fisher, this home is listed in the National Register of Historic Places and has a long documented history that begins before the Civil War. It was noted as haunted after a 2006 renovation, when it was the Caledonia Wine Cottage (2007–9), and many paranormal experiences

75

MISSOURI OZARKS LEGENDS & LORE

were reported at that time. Not only did some folks hear a friendly elderly voice saying hello, but toddlers also played with a girl named Erica that only they could see.

It was originally Stagecoach Inn and then later a twelve-room house with slave quarters and connecting tunnels. It was used as a hospital and prison during the Civil War battle of Pilot Knob, and in time, it was used as part of the Underground Railroad. Later, as an antiques store, it featured stone foundation stairs crafted from the original road, a continuous walnut staircase said to be one of a kind in the Ozarks and an ancient persimmon tree. The building in its current incarnation is known as the Old Caledonian Bed & Breakfast.

Washington County: Potosi, YMCA of the Ozarks

Here's just a side note for YMCA of the Ozarks, featuring the Trout Lodge & Camp Lakewood. The YMCA has a small number of exclusive lodges scattered around the country, and the Potosi lodge, located in the Mark Twain Forest, is one of them! Other lodges include the Silver Bay YMCA at Lake George in the Adirondack Mountains of New York and Frost Valley YMCA, which is set in a renovated turn-of-the-century country estate in the Catskills. There is one in Hawaii as well as some in several international locations.

Chapter 9

HAUNTS AND CURIOSITIES OF THE SPRINGFIELD PLATEAU

S outhwest Missouri—home to Branson, Joplin and Springfield—delivers up some intriguing places along the crossroads of betwixt and between, neither here nor there. Join me to time-travel through the Ozarks by way of Old Route 66. Perhaps we'll meet a Branson haunt, encounter the Joplin Spook Light or run into some Springfield haunts. Anything is possible on the Paranormal Highway, augmented as it is by Ozark limestone, water and iron ore.

GREENE COUNTY

Springfield, Haunted Central High School

423 East Central Street, Springfield, MO 65802

Springfield Central High School is rumored to exist atop open caves that open into Doling Park on the north side of town. A system of cave tunnels originating from the Doling Cave run under north Springfield—tunnels that were supposedly part of the Underground Railroad. Local legend claims that during the Underground Railroad years, escaping slaves were caught and hanged in the cave, and you can still hear their eerie screams in the school's basement.

Missouri Ozarks Legends & Lore

Springfield Haunted Drury University
900 North Benton Avenue, Springfield, MO 65802

The Drury School seems spring-loaded for paranormal activity, given how pianos in the music hall play on their own accord. Not only had the grounds been an old Indian burial ground and location of a bloody Civil War battle, but this was also the location of a Victorian home that burned to the ground. A girl in a pink dress, thought to be the child who perished in the fire, is seen in the Drury School dormitory.

Springfield Haunted Landers Theatre
311 East Walnut Avenue, Springfield, MO

Like many old theaters, the Landers Theatre has an impressive list of paranormal activity. Orbs are seen inside the theater, and from the street a tall blond woman in Elizabethan-style clothing can be seen peering out of a fourth-floor window. Typically, the Lander's balcony has its own haunts, including a circa 1920s janitor. A baby who was accidentally dropped from the balcony a long time ago can be heard crying in the empty theater.

Springfield Haunted Phelps Grove Park
950 East Bennett Street, Springfield, MO 65807

A bride was killed on her wedding day as she and her new husband drove their car through Phelps Grove Park. The faceless ghostly bride is seen in the park at the third bridge in the evening, holding up the hem of her wedding dress.

Springfield Haunted Pythian Castle
1451 East Pythian Street, Springfield, MO

The Paranormal Task Force and Ozark Paranormal Society have certified Pythian Castle as a haunted site. Built by the Knights of Pythias as an

MISSOURI OZARKS LEGENDS & LORE

Pythian Castle has been certified by Paranormal Task Force and Ozark Paranormal Society as a haunted site. *Courtesy of Wikimedia Commons.*

orphanage in 1913, it was later owned by the U.S. military for more than fifty years. The nearly forty thousand square feet of interior space contains more than fifty rooms, including dungeons and a ballroom.

One-hour tours are offered daily. Murder-mystery dinners, comedy nights and ghost tours occur regularly. This twentieth-century landmark building harbors long-deceased residents that evidently never moved out. For the moxie-laden, best to dust off your ghost meter and head to Springfield's only official ghost tour, with an option to overnight it with the Paranormal Task Force ghost hunt.

Springfield, Haunted Springfield National Cemetery

1792 East Seminole Street, Springfield, MO

The Springfield National Cemetery registry lists Revolutionary War soldiers, as well as hundreds of Civil War soldiers who were killed during the Battles of Pea Ridge, Wilson's Creek and Springfield. Amid the final resting place of these fallen soldiers, floating orbs and glowing gravestones have been photographed.

MISSOURI OZARKS LEGENDS & LORE

Springfield, Haunted University Plaza Hotel

333 South John Q Hammons Parkway, Springfield, MO 65806

Even though the University Plaza Hotel is a modern hotel and convention center, it is built on land that had been a plantation owned by an honored Civil War hero who apparently has not moved on yet. Dressed in black, he roams the ballroom and back hallways between midnight and 4:00 a.m.

Springfield, World's Tallest Fork

2215 West Chesterfield Boulevard, Springfield, MO

A lighthearted roadside attraction is worthy of a side trip off the beaten path. Really, who wouldn't be tempted by the world's largest rocking chair, or the world's largest ball of twine, or even a witch's grave? Such is the world's tallest fork in Springfield, Missouri. The offbeat giant fork, once located outside a restaurant, was relocated by Noble & Associates as a sculptural motif outside its offices; the ad agency represents food service and the retail industry. At thirty-five feet tall and weighing eleven tons, the fork angles up toward a three-story building occupied by Noble & Associates, a Springfield ad agency connected to the food service and retail industry. In context, the fork makes sense. A plaque at its base claims that it is the world's largest fork, or at least it was in 1998, when the plaque was installed.

Author's note: This is not to be confused with Branson's Giant Meatball and Fork, featuring a fifteen-foot-diameter walk-through meatball speared on a forty-foot-tall fork. It is located outside Pasghetti's Italian Restaurant on West 76 Country Boulevard; look for the landmark giant tomato and green pepper stuck to the building.

Missouri Ozarks Legends & Lore

Jasper County

I have found out there ain't no surer way to find out whether you like people or hate them than to travel with them.
—*Mark Twain,* Tom Sawyer Abroad

Route 66

As you drive along iconic Route 66 between Waynesville and Joplin, notice the limestone bluffs flanking the highway at Hooker's Cut. These exposed bluffs are actually limestone sediment bedrock, millions of years old, that formed when the area was an inland sea.

Route 66 got its start at a meeting at Springfield, Missouri's Colonial Hotel, making Springfield the birthplace of Route 66. Now, any road with an actual birthplace is likely to have had a visionary creator, and for Route 66, it is Cyrus Avery. Cyrus, known as the father of Route 66, was heavily involved from concept to creation. He not only named the iconic highway

Vintage linen postcard, circa 1930–45, of iconic Route 66, showing sedimentary limestone that formed when the area was an inland sea. Hooker's Cut is located between Waynesville and Rolla, Missouri. *Author's collection.*

18

MISSOURI OZARKS LEGENDS & LORE

but also created the U.S. Highway 66 Association in order to pave and promote it.

Route 66 was developed to connect Chicago to Los Angeles and provide travelers with one-of-a-kind driving experiences. This included must-see roadside attractions like the first fast-food drive-through window at Red's Giant Hamburg in Springfield, as well as many more pieces of preserved Americana along the way.

Carthage, Historic Boots Court Motel

107 South Garrison Avenue, Carthage, MO 64836

The Boots Court Motel, listed in the National Register of Historic Places, sits at the crossroads of the historic Route 66 and U.S. Highway 71 in Carthage, Missouri. The betwixt-and-between crossroads location near Joplin has the desirable but mysterious energy that is likely to support paranormal activity. That translates to making sure to look for anomalies in your photographs—things like orbs or inexplicable traces of light or perhaps an apparition, which are often overlooked or mistaken as camera glitches.

Built in 1939, Boots Court Motel is of the Streamline Moderne style, an international style of Art Deco architecture and design that emerged in the

Boots Court Motel, circa 1939, is listed in the National Register of Historic Places. The design style, Streamline Moderne, emphasizes curved forms and horizontal lines. *Courtesy of Wikimedia Commons, Tony Hisgett, photographer.*

82

Missouri Ozarks Legends & Lore

1930s. Inspired by aerodynamic design, Streamline architecture emphasizes curved forms and horizontal lines. In industrial design, the style was used in railroad locomotives, telephones, buses, appliances and devices to give the impression of sleek modernity.

Original owner Arthur Boots was once a machinery salesman and chose this spot at the crossroads of America. This location, in tandem with modern amenities, made the motel a huge success that attracted the likes of Clark Gable. The motel offered a radio in every room and a private covered carport.

After decades of its successful run, the motel went through a period of decline. An attempt to demolish it in 2003 was halted by protests from locals. Then, in 2011, two sisters prone to renovation purchased Boots. They restored the vintage Route 66 landmark neon sign and the architectural neon light that accentuates the curved horizontal roof line of the vintage building, and they revived rooms to their original décor. As with the original, this twentieth-century motel offers a radio in every room, but no television.

Joplin Phenomena

Truth is stranger than fiction, but it is because fiction is obliged
to stick to possibilities; truth isn't.
—*Mark Twain*

Joplin's crossroads location lives up to its liminality folklore that claims crossroads energy as neither here nor there. Situated in southwest Missouri along Interstate 44, or old Route 66, the Missouri area borders three states: Arkansas, Oklahoma and Kansas. Likewise, Joplin sits at the crosswords, which in mythology represents a location between worlds where supernatural spirits are contacted and paranormal events can take place.

Not only is Joplin located along the Trail of Tears, but its location along the Tornado Alley path also attracted a slice of legendary Bonnie and Clyde lore, who rolled into town quietly and left hastily in a blaze of gunfire, leaving behind jewelry and a camera containing film of personal photographs. The mysterious Joplin Spook Light, which was witnessed as far back as during the Trail of Tears, still appears nightly on a remote four-mile stretch of gravel road known as the Devil's Promenade.

83

MISSOURI OZARKS LEGENDS & LORE

Joplin is known as "the Town that Jack Built," a reference to zinc, which was often referred to as "jack." Joplin was first put on the map by the discovery of lead, but it was zinc that built the town. With the railroads passing through, Joplin became the hub of southwest Missouri and the lead and zinc capital of the world.

No doubt Joplin's location sets the stage for its legend and lore. The Trail of Tears, Joplin Spook Lights and Bonnie and Clyde's legendary and chaotic stay-over all add to its crossroads eerie mystique.

Joplin Spook Light Phenomena

A paranormal enigma for more than a century, the Spook Light was first seen by Indians along the infamous Trail of Tears in 1836, according to legend. An 1881 publication called *The Ozark Spook Light* is the first official documentation of the light.

The Spook Light is often described as an orange orb or ball of fire varying in size from baseball to basketball. It has been seen dancing and spinning, or traveling at high speeds down the center of the gravel road dubbed the Devil's Promenade, and rising and hovering above the treetops before retreating and disappearing. It is also seen swaying from side to side, like a lantern carried by an invisible force. Sightings of the Spook Light are common, sometimes appearing inside vehicles (yikes), and people claim to have felt the heat of the ball as it passed near them.

The Joplin Spook Light, also known as the Hornet Spook Light or the Tri-State Spook Light, is a paranormal enigma for reasons specific to its location. The light is actually located in Oklahoma, near the small town of Quapaw, but is seen from Joplin, Missouri, which is east of Quapaw. This area is marked by an intense crossroads energy and additionally by what is known as the Paranormal Highway, a newly defined reference along the 37th parallel, known for unusual paranormal activity.

Although many paranormal and scientific investigators have studied the phenomenon, including the U.S. Army Corps of Engineers, no one has been able to provide a conclusive answer as to its origin. Many theories have been presented over the years to explain the Joplin Spook Light. One idea is that the light is natural gas escaping from underground, but this theory, which is common in marshy areas, doesn't hold up considering the light is not affected by wind or rain. Another idea is that the light is a reflection created by car lights, but this explanation is easily discarded because the light was seen

84

MISSOURI OZARKS LEGENDS & LORE

years before a road or automobiles existed. Another explanation involves something called will-o'-the-wisps, a luminescence created by rotting organic matter. However, this is debunked because this biological phenomenon does not display the intensity of light as seen with the Joplin Spook Light along the Devil's Promenade.

While these explanations fall short, there is a plausible possibility: shifting rocks below the earth's surface create electrical atmospheric charges that manifest as light.

One ghostly explanation tells of the fate of a Quapaw Indian maiden. When her father would not allow her to marry a young brave, the lovers eloped. When they were tracked by a party of warriors and nearly captured, they joined hands and leaped into the Spring River to their deaths. Shortly thereafter, the light began to appear and is attributed to the spirits of the young lovers.

Another legend tells of a miner who returned to his cabin after being away hunting, only to find it ransacked and his wife and children missing. He continues looking for them, searching the old road known as the Devil's Promenade with the light of his lantern.

To get to the location of the Joplin Spook Light, take I-44 Exit 4—Highway 86 South. Follow about six miles to junction Route BB. Turn right on BB Highway and follow the road until it ends. Turn right again, go one mile and turn left on E50 Road (also known as Spooklight Road). About one and a half to two miles down is the darkest and best place to wait. According to locals, the best time to view the Spook Light is between the hours of 10:00 p.m. and midnight.

BARRY COUNTY: THE RALPH FOSTER MUSEUM, COLLEGE OF THE OZARKS

237 Christian Street, Barry County, Point Lookout, MO 65726

Located on the campus of the College of the Ozarks, the Ralph Foster Museum began in the 1920s and became one of the Midwest's foremost institutions of historical preservation.

The mission of the Ralph Foster Museum is to collect, preserve, interpret and exhibit items relating to the Ozarks region. For many years, Foster collected Native American artifacts, and his interest in the College of the Ozarks prompted him to turn this collection over to the school's museum. Foster

85

MISSOURI OZARKS LEGENDS & LORE

TANEY COUNTY

Branson: Branson Haunts and Curiosities

It's time to track some of Branson's lingering residents. For starters, the late twentieth-century actor Cameron Mitchell is said to haunt Branson wearing a dark suit and ogling tourists through shop windows.

Old downtown Branson offers guided paranormal-themed tours that highlight a bank robber who haunts the train depot. It features wraiths that roam the cemetery and profiles a haunted bed-and-breakfast with transparent guests.

Branson: Haunted Inspiration Point

Inspiration Point has the reputation for rousing a spectral Civil War soldier who flees on horseback during productions of the *Shepherd of the Hills* amphitheater program.

Branson: Lost Canyon Cave, Bat Bar

150 Top of the Rock Road, Taney County, Ridgedale, MO 65739

I love a drink, but I never encouraged drunkenness by harping on its alleged funny side.
—*Mark Twain, Abroad with Mark Twain and Eugene Field*

The Ozark bar in Branson, Missouri, known as Bat Bar gives new credence to the term "watering hole." It's a paradise, complete with a waterfall, located inside a mountaintop cave.

98

Missouri Ozarks Legends & Lore

To achieve nirvana, all you need do is park at the Top of the Rock welcome center and then secure a golf cart to drive and meander through a 2.5-mile woodland path over streams and bridges, where you can stop at a butterfly garden and Eagle Pass scenic overlook. All this before the trail dips into Lost Canyon Cave, wherein lies the magic of its one-of-a-kind bar. Your own personal golf cart is your seating option when you park at the wood bar, where a paint-splashed board reads "Better Settle Your Nerves."

Once you're good and liquored up on cocktails from John L's Hoop-de-Hoo (vodka, tonic and grapefruit), the Cannonball (amaretto, bourbon and pineapple juice), Bat's Blood (vodka with strawberry and peach lemonade) or beer/wine—and after you've signed a liability waiver—it's time to steer that golf cart through Lost Canyon Cave. The path is home to a natural waterfall, a live bat colony, skeletons of a saber-tooth tiger and a short-faced bear.

At irony's best, visitors aren't allowed to walk in the cave, but a railed pathway snakes around the waterfall pool at the heart of the lantern-lit cave. If the cocktails get the best of you, or if the alcohol churns your stomach when paired with bats and skeletons, nearby Big Cedar Lodge is an option for the weaker of our species to sober up.

Branson: Noland Road

A drive down Noland Road, a few miles outside Branson, gets the adrenaline flowing when small handprints show up in the dust on your vehicle. On a dry day, head north on West 76 Country Boulevard and then right onto Old 76 until it Ts with Noland Road on the right. Noland becomes Sycamore Church Road and junctions with Highway 248. Heading south and turning right onto Gretna Road takes you back town.

Branson: Ripley's Believe It or Not! And the World's Largest Ball of Twine
76 Country Boulevard #3326, Branson, MO 65616

You can't depend on your eyes when your imagination is out of focus.
—*Mark Twain*

In the lore of roadside attractions, the phrase "giant twine ball" is catnip, as weighty as a witch's cauldron and as magic as the crossroads of bizarre and obsession.

Missouri Ozarks Legends & Lore

Get yourself over to the Ripley's Believe It or Not! museum in Branson, Missouri—not to be confused with the World's Largest Ball of String elsewhere in Missouri. Now, you might notice that the disheveled, lopsided building that is Ripley's Believe It or Not! appears to be falling down. Not to worry—it is this way on purpose, and was actually spared by the 2012 tornado. One theory for its survival is that the massive twine ball fortified the museum when the tornado whirled through town. Ripley's is home to the usual oddities, such as the ubiquitous two-headed calf and a full-size stagecoach crafted from toothpicks.

All this, not to mention the world's largest roll of toilet paper, is mere backdrop to the twine ball that makes the place unique. The ramshackle building was built around the twine ball, and they'd have to tear it down to get the ball of twine out. The multicolored ball made of plastic bailing twine paves the museum path to an exhibition immortalizing the guy who could hold three golf balls in his mouth.

According to Elsie Payne, wife of the late J.C. Payne, the retired Texas brick mason who rolled the twine ball, it began as a way for J.C. to get his extra hay bale twine out of the way of his cows, who otherwise might have eaten it. One day, J.C.'s son brought to his father's attention a newspaper article that mentioned that the world's largest twine ball (12 feet tall) was in Darwin, Minnesota. Well, J.C. was an ambitious man whose wife claims that he always had to have something to do—he couldn't sit around twiddling his thumbs. J.C. figured that he could beat that record, and so from 1987 to 1991, he gathered all the twine he could (from neighboring ranches and dairies) and rolled a ball 13.5 feet tall. He named it Cloria Crew, of course, had it certified by Guinness as the World's Largest and in 1993 sold it to Ripley's for a rumored $25,000. J.C. went on to roll the World's Largest Ball of Barbed Wire, a contrary orb he was still working on when he died in 2004.

As it goes in the dog-eat-dog world of art, J.C.'s twine ball has its share of critics. From Darwin, Minnesota, critics say that J.C. had help, but Elsie said that J.C. really did roll it all by himself. From Cawker City, Kansas, critics dismissed it as an inferior plastic string ball, whereas Cawker City's ball is made of old-fashioned brown sisal twine. Most harshly, it's hinted that Guinness certified J.C.'s ball merely because it was colorful. Others mention that J.C.'s ball weighs only thirteen thousand pounds, far less than any of the other giant twine balls. That suggests that J.C., being a cheater, wound his ball loose just to make it bigger. But what really upsets twine ball purists the most, however, is believing that J.C.'s obsession with gaining the world record was more important to him than the ball itself. While other Giant

88

MISSOURI OZARKS LEGENDS & LORE

Twine Balls represent labors of love that spanned decades, J.C. supposedly rolled his ball in a mere five years just to sell it to a corporate museum roadside attraction that would stick it in with a bunch of other stuff. It's all documented on the Roadside America website.

Branson: Branson Scenic Railway

Branson Depot, 206 East Main Street, Historic Downtown Branson

Originally known as the White River Railway, circa 1902, the Branson Scenic Railway now operates as a heritage railway, meaning it operates as living history with the purpose of re-creating and preserving railway scenes of the past. Your rail journey begins at the historic (circa 1905) Branson Depot in downtown Branson, now the Branson Scenic Railway's headquarters. Next you'll board the Ozark Zephyr, a vintage, diesel-powered locomotive with circa 1930–60 restored cars. With no assigned seating, passengers are free to wander from car to car. Three dome cars boast outstanding panoramic views of the lush countryside, rolling hills and observable wildlife, along with sights while the train is going through original trestles and tunnels. Concessions are available, as well as expert guides who point out wildlife, scenery and historic landmarks along the way. If you like ghost towns, old bridges and railroad trestles, this is the venue for you. Choose from two separate routes that each are about forty miles round-trip.

The underlying rail lines are owned by Missouri and Northern Arkansas Railroad, which is still active and therefore has the right-of-way on the tracks. The Missouri and Northern Arkansas Railroad schedule, along with freight trains using the same tracks, determines whether the Branson Scenic Railway will operate tours headed north or south.

Branson: The Haunted Titanic Museum

3235 76 Country Boulevard, Branson, MO 65616

Get your facts first, then you can distort them as you please.
—*Mark Twain*

The Titanic Museum accounts for haunts by crew members who have reported fingerprints that won't go away with repeated cleanings. Wet bare footprints with no apparent source are common, and transparent guests dressed in formal clothing are seen strolling its corridors.

MISSOURI OZARKS LEGENDS & LORE

OZARK PARANORMAL HIGHWAY

The 37th Parallel Band

Chuck Zukowski's theory of the 37th parallel invokes a decisive response to those who consider it, one way or the other. In the context of the Ozarks, most everything he presents inherently occurs in the Missouri and Arkansas Ozarks. Consider the many UFO sightings, seismic events, natural formations like caves and sink holes, man-made structures such as military bases and sacred Native Americans sites.

The 37th parallel north is a band of latitude that is 37 degrees north of Earth's equator. This band comprises the 37th parallel, bordered by the 38th to the north and 36th to the south. The Ozark area between 36th and 38th is a largely uninhabited stretch of land where mysterious things happen with unnerving frequency.

In North America, the band stretches across the heartland. From east to west, it goes through Virginia, Kentucky, Arkansas, Missouri and Kansas. It then passes through the Four Corners region that divides Colorado, New Mexico, Utah and Arizona. It continues west through Nevada, ending at San Francisco, California. The Missouri Ozark's Salem and Springfield Plateaus sit comfortably inside the band.

Chuck Zukowski, Researcher

Chuck Zukowski was dubbed the Colorado UFO nut, and he's proud of the label. He's been researching paranormal events for more than twenty-five years, specifically UFO sightings, alien abductions, cattle mutilations and other strange phenomena across the United States, as documented on the UFO Nut website.

Zukowski first noticed a linear pattern emerge in Colorado and then in other locations along the 37th parallel. He began mapping reports of UFO sightings, abductions and mutilations—paired with locations of caves, military basis and sacred sites. He pieced together reports of UFO sightings on the 37th degree latitude and developed a theory of possible underground bases throughout Missouri's massive cave system.

Zukowski's theory, in a nutshell, considers the possibility of underground alien bases that exist in the network of caves along the 37th parallel, such as the massive cave systems in Kentucky, Oklahoma, Arizona, Missouri

MISSOURI OZARKS LEGENDS & LORE

and Arkansas. These cave systems offer structural stabilization and water sourced from underground streams.

All this, along with man-made structures along the parallel, is the basis of the theory. The top-secret base Area 51 is on the parallel, as are Fort Knox and the Pentagon. Earthquakes occur along the parallel, such as the 1811–12 New Madrid, Missouri quakes; the 1906 San Francisco earthquake; and the 2011 Fukushima, Japan disaster. UFO sightings and a few crashes are well documented. Notable UFO crashes along the parallel include the Ozark 1941 crash at Cape Girardeau, Missouri; the 1947 crash in Roswell, New Mexico, which is considered the holy grail of UFO folklore; and the 1948 crash at Aztec, New Mexico.

Thousands of cows and horses have been found mysteriously drained of their blood along this stretch. Reproductive organs, tongues and ears were removed with eerie surgical accuracy, leaving cauterized wounds. Oddly, the earth surrounding the gruesome scene is always left completely undisturbed. It's as if the mutilated animal were dropped from the sky.

Chapter 10
OZARK WITCHCRAFT

You believe in a book that has talking animals, wizards, witches, demons, sticks turning into snakes, burning bushes, food falling from the sky, people walking on water, and all sorts of magical, absurd and primitive stories, and you say that we are the ones that need help?
—*Mark Twain*

An old saying claims that still waters run deep, an' the devil lies at the bottom. The notion of witchcraft is deeply embedded in traditional Ozark folklore. But the Ozarker will not admit their belief in witchcraft to someone they don't know. Even with a deep-seated belief and experiences in everyday life, the tradition is to deny all knowledge of it.

When it comes to discussing witchcraft, the old sayin's and conjure words must be learned from a member of the opposite sex. Doctrines are passed only between blood relatives or people who have had sexual intercourse. Every witch obtains her unholy wisdom from a lover or a male relative.

However, a mother can transmit the secrets to her son, and he can pass it to his wife. She tells a male cousin, and so on in a circular loop. People who know the secrets are regarded as carriers but must use the deadly formulae to become a genuine witch. Thus, knowledge of witchcraft that exists in certain families and clans can lie dormant for a long time.

Initiation Rituals

Folklore stemming from Galena, Missouri, claims that a woman may simply fire a silver bullet at the moon and mutter two or three obscene sayin's. From Barry County, Missouri, folklore claims that any woman who repeats the Lord's Prayer backward and fires seven silver bullets at the moon is transformed into a witch "instanter."

A darker side of ritual claims that a woman who decides to become a witch must be a virgin and must participate in a ritual whereby she goes to the family buryin' ground at midnight, in the dark of the moon. There, she verbally renounces the Christian religion and swears to give herself body and soul to the devil.

She removes her clothing, which she hangs on an infidel's tombstone, and then delivers her body to the devil's ambassador—that is, the man who is inducing her into the mystery. With the sex act completed, both recite terrible words to conjure devils and spirits of the evil non-dead, according to Randolph's *Ozark Magic and Folklore*. This is followed by reciting the Lord's Prayer backward. All of this must be witnessed by at least two nude initiates, and the ritual must be repeated three consecutive nights. After the first and second vows, the candidate is still free to change her mind; however, the third pledge is final. Once the third pledge is complete, the witch must serve the devil throughout eternity.

Witch

In Ozark witchcraft folklore a witch is always a woman who has sold her soul to the devil in order to gain supernatural power. Ozark old-timers agree it's rather complicated to become a witch, and there is more than one way to achieve it. But all agree that the devil is the root cause of it and that a hocus-pocus ritual is required to finalize the deal.

Discrepancies are easily noted in the various initiation rituals. On the one hand, the witch wannabe must be a young virgin; on the other hand, she can be a widow or old spinster. Now, that just doesn't add up in my book. Elsewhere, witches are notably women who receive their power and initiation from men with whom they must have sexual intercourse. What woman with half a brain would fall for that? Later, when they realize they'd been duped, what would keep them from putting a boatload of curses on their perpetrators?

Witch Masters

However, some witches claim that their spells are directed against the forces of evil, and they remove spells and curses cast on their clients by supernatural means, such as dark witches. These practitioners who represent the good side of witchcraft are known as witch masters, white witches, witch doctors, faith doctors, goomer doctors and conjure folks.

Witches' Magical Powers

Witches can make themselves invisible, as everybody knows, but there is one method by which anybody can see them. All that's necessary is to throw a pinch of dust from a puffball, known as the devil's snuffbox, into a whirlwind.

A witch can assume the form of any bird or animal, but cats and wolves are their favorite disguises.

A witch can cast spells on people, places, animals, crops, livestock and weather—all causing sickness and pain. A witch's spell is almost always intended to do harm or cause chaos and suffering.

Ways to Ward Off Witches

It seems that there are as many Ozark ways to ward off witches as there are ways to cure a person of warts. Here are a few suggestions should you find yourself in a curious predicament.

Painting the outside of an exterior door will ward off witches.

You might consider nailing the entrails of a horned owl or the genitals of a male fox over that door. No? Perhaps your aesthetic sensibility is more in harmony with fastening deer horns over the door or placing two hazel wood sticks on the wall in the shape of a cross. This method also works in barns to protect your cattle and horses from disease. Continuing the concept of crosses, some of the old folks would set up the mop and broom so as to form a cross to keep witches out of the house. However, if called on that, they'd deny that it was to ward off witches—rather, it was to keep somebody from walking on a clean floor.

Now, if you have nothing to lose regarding your reputation, run three times around the cabin at dusk while shaking a white rag above your head. No? Perhaps creating an egg tree is more your cup of tea. To do this, take a dead bush with its branches trimmed and then cover it with hundreds of egg shells that have been carefully blown—whatever that means.

A Hot Springs man claimed that he could stop supernatural evil-doing by repeating aloud, "Old Tom Walker under your hat, Bound in the name of God the Father, God the Son, and God the Holy Spirit."

Another phrase to repeat when you need a victory goes like this: "God the Father is with me. God the Son may be with thee. The Holy Ghost is with us all. But I will rise, and you will fall."

Adopting certain gestures to use while repeating catchphrases will enhance their power, such as clasping your hands together with thumbs crossed in the "King's X." Holding the right thumb in the left hand and the left thumb in the right hand works well for the ambidextrous.

If these methods fail, get a witch master—a Glinda the Good Witch, if you will—especially one gifted to draw a picture of the bad witch and fire a silver bullet into it. Another option is to find a witch killer, someone who will make an image of the bad witch out of mud and then drive nails into it or beat it with a hammer or burn it. Problem solved.

Ways to Ward Off Witches from a Child

To protect a child from witches, have the boy or girl wear a necklace of dried burdock roots cut into small pieces and stranded like a beaded necklace. Now, if this child gets bewitched anyway, stand him or her on their head while you count to forty-nine backward. This removes the curse.

When a bewitched infant cries constantly, carry the child to the front door every morning for nine consecutive days. You must lick its face from the nose to the hairline. Then, on the ninth day, the offending witch will appear at the door and ask to borrow something. Refusing her request will break the spell forever.

Chapter 11

IRON COUNTY

Distance lends enchantment to the view.
—*Mark Twain,* Eruption

Iron County's nearly 552 square miles, 550 are land and 1.8 are water. The county has two areas that are nationally protected: Mark Twain National Forest and Pilot Knob National Wildlife Refuge.

The county is located west of the Mississippi River in an area known as the Lead Belt region of Missouri, Salem Plateau of southeast Missouri. Iron County was organized on February 17, 1857, and gets its name based on the abundance of iron ore found within its borders. Iron ore deposits are found in sedimentary rocks, where they are formed from chemical reactions of iron and oxygen in water, either fresh or marine. Minerals in these deposits are the iron oxides hematite and magnetite. Iron of meteoric origin contains nickel. Iron is inherently remarkable because it is created in the core of imploding red super-giant stars, meaning elements form together inside a star during fusion. When a supernova occurs, newly created iron fragments are blasted into space, where they float around for millions of years before landing on a planet and beginning the process of becoming iron oxide.

Now, if this motivates someone to march right down to the nearest Walmart and purchase a cast-iron skillet to cook up some cornbread using Grandma's recipe, well, I'll just say you wouldn't be the first.

Iron County—with its observable complement of iron ore, limestone sedimentary rock and moving water—has the perfect combination of earth

Missouri Ozarks Legends & Lore

elements for attracting and supporting what we consider to be paranormal activity. Likewise, considering that our blood is the color red because of its iron content, this lends credence to the notion that we are star dust, after all, and that perhaps Iron County, Missouri, is a magical place.

Bear with this Missouri native, an upshot of the Show Me State attempting to grasp how the St. Francois Mountains exist independent of the Ozark Mountains yet stand together in time and space in the Missouri Ozarks. First thing, the St. Francois Mountains formed of igneous volcanic rock possibly 4.5 billion years ago. Second, the Ozark plateau formed of sedimentary rock over millions of years. This means that the St. Francois Mountains already existed when an inland sea created sedimentary bedrock around them, bedrock that became the Ozark Mountains when uplift occurred. Got it!

Arcadia Valley

The six-mile-long and two-mile-wide stretch known as Arcadia Valley in Iron County is surrounded by the St. Francois Mountains. Three towns are located in the valley: Arcadia, Ironton and Pilot Knob.

Arcadia Academy

Arcadia Academy has been towering over the Arcadia Valley for more than 150 years, a slice of Ozark history that is listed in the National Register of Historic Districts. Built in 1846, the academy's architecture, which includes two hundred rooms, is some of the most beautiful in the entire state of Missouri, and the chapel's stained-glass windows are world class. A unique roof truss system designed in Germany is the crown jewel of the gymnasium. This circa 1846 building began as a Methodist high school and has had many incarnations. By 1847, it had become the prestigious Arcadia High School. Families moved here so their children could attend the new wilderness school of higher learning, and by 1859, there were 109 boys and 66 girls enrolled.

In 1861, the school was forced to close during the Civil War when Union forces occupied the area and used it as a hospital until 1863. When it reopened as a school in 1863, the roster showed that tuition was ten dollars, board was sixteen dollars and washing, lodging and fuel totaled eighty dollars.

97

Arcadia Academy, circa 1846, is listed in the National Register of Historic Districts. It has been a school, a Civil War hospital and a bed-and-breakfast. Known for paranormal activity, anomalies sometime show up in photographs. *Courtesy of Wikimedia Commons, Skyrunner75.*

In 1877, Ursuline nuns purchased the school for $30,000 and turned it into an all-girls school. St. Joseph's Chapel was built in 1907, and a four-story wing was added in 1913. The 1870 building burned later in 1913 and the school closed in 1971, but the building served as a convent for nuns until 1985.

Arcadia Academy is now a popular vacation destination. The historic bed-and-breakfast has lodging options ranging from suites to cottages, European-style rooms and large family-style rooms. The bakery and boutique store are worthy of a one-hundred-mile day trip from St. Louis, and the Academy's acclaimed Three Abbey Kitchen has a full-service restaurant offering American-style meals, making the kitchen a destination in its own right. Arcadia Academy's auditorium (with stage) seats 250 people and is used as a venue for plays, community theater and weddings. After dark, check out the ghost tour offerings on premise just for fun.

Belleview: Elephant Rocks State Park

7390, 7406 MO-21, Belleview, MO 63623

Elephant Rocks State Park is a state-owned protected geologic reserve located in the St. Francois Mountains. This outcropping of Precambrian granite comprises a string of large granite boulders that resembles a train of pink circus elephants. The 1.5-billion-year-old granite boulders intrigue geologists and history buffs alike and are a destination for the curious.

Ironton

The town of Ironton, known as the Queen City of the Francois Mountains, is the county seat of Iron County. Its 1.39 square miles is home to .05 square miles of water and about 1,500 people. Ironton was designated the county seat in 1857, and the Ironton Post Office has been in operation since 1858. That's a lot to expect from a small town that was named for iron ore deposits found in the vicinity.

During the Civil War, Brigadier General Ulysses S Grant led a force of four Union regiments in the area. In a letter to his wife, he described the

It's notable to mention that a similar outcropping of Precambrian pink granite, known as Enchanted Rock, presents in the Texas Hill Country as a dome that covers 640 acres and rises 425 feet above the surrounding terrain. Both locations have an aura of mysticism and intriguing lore. Enchanted Rock is known to hum after sunset.

Elephant Rocks State Park is one of the most curious geologic sites in Missouri, with an outcropping of 1.5 billion-year-old red granite boulders that resemble a quirky train of circus elephants. *Courtesy of Wikimedia Commons, Fredyfish4.*

MISSOURI OZARKS LEGENDS & LORE

area as one of the most delightful places he'd ever been. That's quite the compliment from a politician who served as the eighteenth president of the United States, albeit the commander of invading forces at the time.

Pilot Knob

Today, the Arcadia Valley in Iron County is a peaceful setting in one of Missouri's most scenic areas. But in September 1864, the valley was the scene of one of the largest, bloodiest and most hard-fought battles waged on the state's soil: the Battle of Pilot Knob. During the battle, Confederate major general Sterling Price led an army of eight thousand men against the Union post of Fort Davidson at Pilot Knob.

The Battle of Pilot Knob State Historic Site preserves Fort Davidson and the battlefield where so many Confederate and Union soldiers lost their lives. A visitors' center and museum interpret the conflict with exhibits, audiovisual presentations and a fiber-optic diorama of the battle.

TAUM SAUK MOUNTAIN STATE PARK

Nature knows no indecencies; man invents them.
—Mark Twain's Notebook

The name of the highest point in the St. Francois Mountains, Taum Sauk, has a layered meaning. It derives from Sauk-Ton-Qua, the Piankeshaw chief, and the word *sauk*, a Native American reference meaning outlet. Not only is Taum Sauk Mountain the highest point, but it is also older than the surrounding Ozark Mountains. As documented by the Britannica website, it is an igneous mountain amid a sedimentary seabed; it jutted out from the surrounding ancient inland sea as an island during the Paleozoic period.

In 1991, the State of Missouri created Taum Sauk Mountain State Park, a 7,448-acre park that is home to the highest point in the state. Included is a rustic campground and a paved trail to the highpoint, as well as a lookout tower for viewing the mountain from a vantage point above its dense forest canopy.

Taum Sauk forests, rocky glades and trails provide solitary experiences for hikers. In addition, the thirty-three-mile Taum Sauk section of the Ozark Trail is rated as one of the best trails in Missouri.

Missouri Ozarks Legends & Lore

While the St. Francois Mountains are an ancient Precambrian igneous uplift several times older than the Appalachians, the rest of the Ozarks are the result of erosion of sedimentary strata. Geologists believe that Taum Sauk is among the few areas in the United States never to have been submerged under ancient seas. Even with its low elevation at 1,772 feet, Taum Sauk and the St. Francois range are true mountains of volcanic origin.

The topography of Taum Sauk Mountain, the highest point in Missouri, is that of an elongated ridge with a north-northwest/south-southeast orientation, rather than a peak. The ranges of the St. Francois Mountains existed as islands in a shallow inland sea throughout most of the Paleozoic era, when sandstone and limestone and shale were deposited all around the older St. Francois Mountains and built up the ocean floor. The process required millions of years, followed by uplift, to form what became the Ozark Mountains.

The Ozark Mountains of the Salem Plateau region, which surround the St. Francois Mountains at their base, are vertical relief and jagged mountains formed by sedimentary strata erosion. Weathering and erosion of these ancient peaks provided the sediments of the surrounding rock layers.

Although Taum Sauk Mountain is the highest mountain in Missouri, it is not the most prominent. Taum Sauk rises 522 feet from an already elevated base. Mudlick Mountain rises 693 feet from a lower base to an elevation of 1,313 feet. Black Mountain, in Madison County, has the highest rise in elevation in Missouri. From its base along the St. Francis River (540 feet above sea level) to its summit (1,503 feet above sea level), Black Mountain rises just under 1,000 feet in elevation from the valley below.

Mina Sauk Falls, the highest waterfall in Missouri, is on Taum Sauk and can be visited by hiking a rugged three-mile round-trip trail loop. Cascading water ranges from a trickle in dry conditions to a full cascading falls after there has been a lot of rain.

Taum Sauk Mountain State Lore

This flat-ridged mountain is likely named after Piankeshaw chief Sauk-Ton-Qua and the legend of his tragic tale. When Mina Sauk, his daughter, fell in love with a warrior from a hostile tribe, the chief killed him and threw him off a cliff, and then Mina followed him over the edge.

This incurred the wrath of the mythical Storm King, as told by Adas Obscura, who in response conjured up a hurricane that wiped out Sauk-Ton-

101

Missouri Ozarks Legends & Lore

Qua's entire tribe. Afterward, a lightning bolt struck the ground, causing the waterfall to appear, and the falls wiped away the blood of the lovers.

Taum Sauk Reservoir and Reservoir Catastrophic Failure

Architects cannot teach nature anything
—*Mark Twain*

In what was an inevitable mind-boggling event, overtopping the water level at the Taum Sauk Upper Storage Facility caused a catastrophic dam failure when a large section of the parapet wall of the upper reservoir failed. This occurred during the predawn hours of December 14, 2005, but given the timing during the off-season, catastrophic loss of human life was thankfully averted.

Near the end of the morning pumping cycle, both the primary reservoir sensors and the fail-safe probes failed to report the critical high water level in the reservoir. The probes had been incorrectly set at a higher level than the low point on the parapet, meaning there was no way to maintain actual reservoir levels and no way to evaluate crest elevation around the reservoir rim regarding shutdown triggers.

Taum Sauk mountaintop reservoir in the St. Francois Mountains. *Courtesy of Wikimedia Commons.*

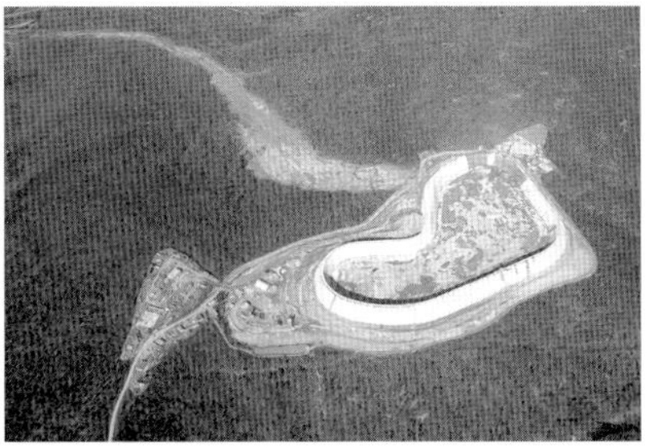

Missouri Ozarks Legends & Lore

As the depth of water in the reservoir increased, the nappe shifted farther away from the reservoir, eroding the exposed and unprotected rockfill embankment supporting the wall. This ultimately caused the 656-foot-wide breach in the dike. When it gave way, more than 1.5 billion gallons of water formed a 20-foot wall that scourged Profit Mountain and flowed into the east fork of the Black River and the lower ground of Johnson's Shut-Ins State Park—all within thirty minutes. This scourging opened the opportunity for geologists to further study the rock content of the mountain.

Taum Sauk Reservoir aerial view. *Courtesy of Wikimedia Commons, Kbh3rd.*

Chapter 12

MADISON COUNTY

A thing long expected takes the form of the unexpected when at last it comes.
—*Mark Twain*, Mark Twain's Notebook

FREDERICKTOWN

My Francis ancestors of the westward expansion settled in Fredericktown during the early 1800s and were among the first to privately own land here. They were farmers who purchased acres incrementally at $1.25 per acre, with the number of acres dependent on the yield of a harvest.

Fredericktown is ninety miles due south of St. Louis and fifty miles northwest of Cape Girardeau and is on the outer boundary of the St. Francois Mountains. All of this natural beauty is surrounded on three sides by the Mark Twain National Forest. Fredericktown was settled in 1819 by French settlers.

The historic Madison County Courthouse, circa 1898, was designed by architect Theodore Link and added to the National Register of Historic Places in 2000. It is a two-story rectangular Lancaster Plan, eclectic Late Victorian brick-and-granite building with an attic and full basement. The courthouse square layout features two streets that extend perpendicular to the central square of the courthouse. The downtown district's commercial section exhibits commercial buildings (circa early 1800s through the 1940s) that range from one to three stories tall. The oldest existing building in the district—a limestone building originally used as a livery stable—was constructed circa 1845.

Missouri Ozarks Legends & Lore

Early settlers came to the area in 1701 seeking gold and silver. What they found was iron ore, lead and copper. By 1799, the land, which was granted by Spain to thirteen French Creole settlers, had become St. Michael's Village. An 1814 flood wiped out the village, and residents moved to higher ground owned by Colonel Nathaniel Cook. Then in 1818, St. Michael's Village was renamed Fredericktown after Colonel George Frederick Bollinger and was incorporated in 1827.

During the 1800s, although Fredericktown was mainly rural, it was a railway hub and commercial center that experienced cycles of economic boom or bust. During the 1900s, early livelihood was based on farming and lead mining until the Great Depression. The Brown Shoe Company brought economic growth that lasted until the 1970s. Brown was Fredericktown's economic mainstay until the railroad stopped operating.

Battle of Fredericktown, Civil War

Our Civil War was a blot on our history, but not as great a blot as the buying and selling of Negro souls.
—*Mark Twain, quoted by Clara Clemens Gabrilowitsch in a letter to the New York Herald Tribune, November 19, 1941*

One example of how Missouri was divided on the issue of slavery, with brothers on both Confederate and Union sides, is the legendary Mark Twain himself. After his brief stint as a Confederate soldier, he headed west with his Unionist brother to see the Wild West. His experiences are captured in his book *Roughing It*.

The Battle of Fredericktown was pivotal because it gave the Union forces control over southeast Missouri. This is how it played out. In October 1861, Confederate general M. Jeff Thompson led a force of three thousand men into southeast Missouri. Then, on October 15, 1861, Thompson led a cavalry attack on the Iron Mountain Railroad bridge over the Big River near Blackwell in Jefferson County. The bridge was burned in order to prevent Union forces from using it, and Thompson retreated to his infantry back in Fredericktown, where strong Union forces were closing in.

Union colonel J.B. Plummer was sent from Cape Girardeau to Fredericktown with about 1,500 soldiers, while Union colonel W.P. Carlin advanced from Pilot Knob with about 3,000 men. Learning that Union forces were approaching from east and west, Confederate general Thompson

105

Battle of Fredericktown: Civil War Narratives

Francis family historian George Linvel Knott (1923–2008), of Frederickrown, was my grandmother's cousin through the Francis line. Anybody who knew George knew how much he loved to talk about family history. In fact, George had a reputation such that you might think twice before getting him wound up because he loved talking, and once he got to talking, he didn't come up for air.

George was part of a team through the Madison County Historical Society that collected and assembled the family histories of Madison County. They were published in 1988 in the book titled *Madison Historical Madison: The History*

began a withdrawal from Fredericktown south along the Greenville Road. By midnight, October 29, General Thompson's forces had marched twelve miles south of Fredericktown. At this point, Thompson decided to return with his infantry to attack Union forces along the road from Fredericktown to Jackson.

Arriving before dawn on October 21, Thompson positioned his forces along the road, but finding that Union soldiers had taken another route slightly north of the main road, he repositioned his battery ambush just south of Fredericktown along the Greenville Road.

It was there on the afternoon of October 21 that the Confederate command was engaged by about half the Union forces sent in pursuit of Thompson. The Union artillery was hauled out, and the Seventeenth Iowa Regiment charged the Confederate battery, capturing one gun. The running battle lasted more than four hours, with the Confederates in halting retreat. Late in the afternoon, the Union troops returned to Fredericktown and reported seven soldiers dead and some sixty wounded.

The next morning, Union soldiers reported burying 160 Confederate dead, although General Thompson put the number of Confederate dead at 20, with thirty captured.

Confederate general Thompson made good his retreat, carrying away about 1,800 pounds of lead taken from Mine La Motte just north of Fredericktown to aid the Confederacy. During the chaos following the battle, Union forces took possession of Fredericktown, firing the town and destroying homes.

Reenactments of the 1863 Civil War battle of Fredericktown and other Civil War living history demonstrations occur every third September.

Missouri Ozarks Legends & Lore

of Madison County, Missouri 1818-1988 by the Heritage and Landmarks Commission and the Madison County Historical Society; Paula Sheley served as the editor. If anyone goes looking for a copy of this book, be aware that the cover title is printed as *Historical Madison County 1818-1989*.

This story originally was told to Alice Francis by William Andrew Kennedy (her grandfather). Alice Francis was George's grandmother (and sister to my great-grandmother Bell Francis) and passed it along to George, who passed it along to me.

The following narrative is based on my conversations with George; however, these narratives are also published in the book. There are two family accounts of my ancestors during the Civil War battle of Fredericktown that I've chosen to include.

William Andrew Kennedy (1827-1899), and His Son, John Kennedy

This family legend places William Andrew Kennedy (great-great-great-grandfather to the author) and his eldest son, John Kennedy, together in the trenches during the Battle of Fredericktown, October 21, 1861.

Father and son joined the Confederate army at Fredericktown and fought in the Battle of Fredericktown. William Andrew told of his son's reaction to the battle. When the first cannonball passed over his head, sixteen-year-old John told his father that he was going to go home. William Andrew grabbed John's arm and pulled him low into the trench. William said to his young son, "Son, once you jump up from this trench, the Feds will cut you to pieces." John stayed for the retreat.

William Andrew Kennedy

William Andrew Kennedy also spoke of his experience during the Civil War, such as when he was one of the first soldiers of his regiment in camp to awaken one cold morning. They slept outdoors in the open air using their military blankets for warmth. When William Andrew Kennedy awoke, he discovered that a blanket of snow had fallen overnight. It slowly accumulated and covered the regiment as they slept. He said that as each soldier arose from under his blanket and the snow fell away, it gave him the impression of the scene on Resurrection Morning when all the dead shall rise.

107

Chapter 13

NEW MADRID THROUGH REYNOLDS COUNTY

I will set it down here as a maxim that the operations of the human intellect are much accelerated by an earthquake. Usually I do not think rapidly—but I did upon this occasion. I thought rapidly, vividly, and distinctly. With the first shock of the fire, I thought—"I recognize that motion—this is an earthquake." With the second, I thought, "What a luxury this will be for the morning papers." With the third shock, I thought, "Well my boy, you had better be getting out of this." Each of these thoughts was only the hundredth part of a second in passing through my mind. There is no incentive to rapid reasoning like an earthquake. I then sidled out toward the middle of the street—and I may say that I sidled out with some degree of activity, too. There is nothing like an earthquake to hurry a man when he starts to go anywhere.

—*Mark Twain*

New Madrid County: New Madrid Earthquakes, 1811–12

The New Madrid earthquakes are the worst in recorded history. No other earthquakes have lasted as long nor produced as much damage as the New Madrid events, and they were felt as far away as New York City, Boston (where church bells rang), Montreal and Washington, D.C. President James Madison and his wife, Dolley, felt the quakes in the White House. From December 16, 1811, through March 1812, there were more than two thousand earthquakes in the central Mississippi Valley, as well

New Madrid, on the banks of the Mississippi River, was the epicenter of 1811–12 earthquakes (the worst ever recorded), which caused the river to run backward for a short time. *Author's collection.*

as between six thousand and ten thousand in the Boot Heel of Missouri. New Madrid, located near the junction of the Ohio and Mississippi Rivers, experienced more than two thousand earthquakes in five months. Three of the quakes were among the most intense ever experienced. The first of the three registered 8.1 on the Richter Scale (December 16, 1811), the second registered 7.8 (January 23, 1812) and the third was an 8.8 (February 7, 1812). Many people went missing and were deemed to have been swallowed up by the earth. Others discovered that most crevices split the ground in a north–south orientation, with some as long as five miles. With that observation, some survivors endured the catastrophe by devising a means of riding out the quake. They'd chop down trees so that they fell in an east–west direction and then hold on to the tree during a quake, using it as a bridge that spanned the north–south fissures as chasms opened.

Many who experienced the earthquakes' intensity and resulting devastation, day after day, believed that it was the end of the world. Here are a few of the reasons why.

Missouri Ozarks Legends & Lore

Mississippi River Ran Backward

After the February 7 earthquake, boatmen who survived on flatboats reported that the Mississippi ran backward for several hours. The force of the land upheaval fifteen miles south of New Madrid created chaos to the extent that Reelfoot Lake spontaneously formed; inhabitants of an Indian village drowned; thousands of acres of virgin forest were destroyed; and two temporary waterfalls appeared in the Mississippi Valley.

Phenomena in Nature

Tecumseh's Comet preceded the quakes. The comet, which had been visible for seventeen months, was brightest during the quakes. Additionally, strange or unnatural animal behavior was reported before the quakes. Overall, animals were restless and nervous. Domestic animals turned wild, and wild animals turned tame. Snakes came out of the ground from hibernation, and flocks of ducks and geese landed in populated areas.

Sand Boils

So much energy was released from the ground during the New Madrid earthquakes that the world's largest sand boil was created. Known as "the beach" by locals, it is located in the Boot Heel of Missouri; it's a sizeable 1.4 miles long and comprises 136 acres.

Sand boils, or sand volcanoes, are harbingers of earthquakes. They occur when water (driven by pressure) seeps up from underground into a bed of sand. The water that reaches the surface appears to be boiling, hence the name. Likewise, seismic tar balls (petroliferous nodules), or solidified petroleum pellets the size of golf balls, are found in sand boils and fissures.

Earthquake Lights

Earthquake lights (seismoluminescence) flashed light into the sky out of the ground because the land in and around New Madrid is rich in quartz crystal. When the quartz is pressurized, it projects light. How frightening this must have been to a civilization unfamiliar with electricity! It was not until 1925 that electricity for residential use was common.

110

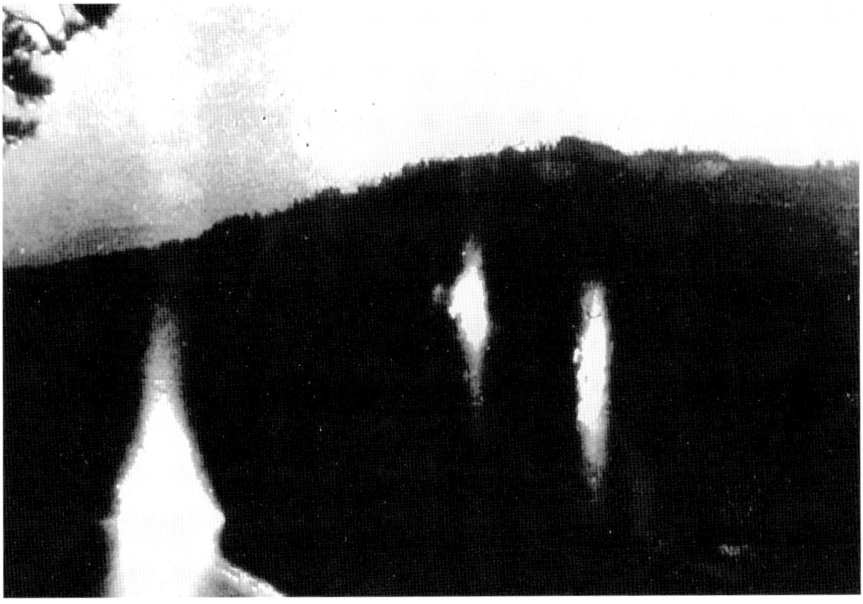

Earthquake lights captured on film during a series of aftershocks. *Courtesy of Seismological Society of America, Seismological Research Letters (SRL/SSA), and Mihai Danica, photographer.*

Sand boils occur during earthquakes when warm water under pressure wells up through a bed of sand. New Madrid saw the largest documented sand boils during the quakes. *Courtesy of Wikimedia Commons, Mikenorton.*

MISSOURI OZARKS LEGENDS & LORE

Warm Water

As if harbingers such as Tecumseh's Comet, sand boils and unnatural animal behavior weren't enough to put people on their last nerve, the water that erupted during these winter earthquakes was lukewarm; it was thought to have been warmed by the earth quaking and/or by quartz light heating the water. One can easily imagine why it seemed like Armageddon.

Explosions

Cryptic rumbling, deafening thunder and explosions accompanied the many quakes. Earthquake smog turned the daytime skies so dark that even lighted lamps couldn't penetrate it. The air smelled bad, laden with dust particles created by warm water erupting into winter's cold air, and it was difficult to breathe.

Comic Relief

It seems that the city of New Madrid, with its history of natural disaster and war, has maintained a sense of humor, as shown in the photograph here, taken on the greenspace at the courthouse. During the peak of fall color, this display features not just one Halloween witch but rather an entire coven.

A capricious witches coven was the fall decoration at the New Madrid Courthouse, October 2019. *Author's collection.*

MISSOURI OZARKS LEGENDS & LORE

NEW MADRID COUNTY, NEW MADRID:
THE STEAMBOAT *NEW ORLEANS*

The steamboat *New Orleans* was the first steamboat to travel on the Ohio and Mississippi Rivers. The river voyage occurred during the New Madrid earthquakes, and yet it survived the quakes while on the water. Frankly, the timing was terrible.

Captain Nicholas Roosevelt along with his young wife, Lydia; two-year-old daughter; and their Labrador dog named Tiger set out from Pittsburgh on October 20, 1811, bound for New Orleans. Ten days after leaving Pittsburgh, Lydia gave birth to a son in Louisville, Kentucky. They docked and waited about six weeks for her to recover. The timing was in sync for the water at the Falls of the Ohio to rise, where dangerous waters and coral reefs awaited travelers when the water was too low.

On December 16, one night before the earthquakes began, the steamboat anchored near Owensboro, Kentucky, on the Ohio River, about two hundred miles east of New Madrid, Missouri. Their Labrador insisted on staying in the cabin with them instead of sleeping on the deck. Tiger sensed trouble, and for good reason. Without realizing it, Captain Nicholas Roosevelt and his charges were heading straight toward the epicenter of the greatest earthquake in recorded history.

At Henderson, Kentucky, where no chimneys were left standing, they stopped to visit the painter John James Audubon and his wife, Lucy. Floating in the middle of the Ohio River, they were protected from the earthquake tremors shaking the land, but not from the hazards of fallen trees floating down steam, disappearing islands and collapsing riverbanks.

The unfamiliar sight of the steamboat *New Orleans*, which was intended to be a visual and tangible advertisement for steam travel, was interpreted instead to be the cause of the earthquake by many who saw it. After the ship entered Indian Territory on December 18, two days after the quake, Indians who figured that the "fire canoe" had caused the earthquake chased it, but couldn't catch it. That same night, the cabin caught fire. Even though the crew managed to extinguish the fire, they had to have feared what else might go wrong.

Thousands of fallen trees were floating on the waters of the Mississippi as they approached New Madrid on December 19, three days after the earthquake. When they found that the town of New Madrid had been destroyed, they didn't dare to stop and pick up survivors. Not only were they incapable of assistance, but their provisions were also depleted; they feared being overtaken by a desperate mob.

113

Missouri Ozarks Legends & Lore

Most alarming was the fact that in addition to the chaos they witnessed along the banks of the Mississippi River, they had not seen a boat ascending the river in three days. They saw only wrecked and abandoned boats but kept on going south toward New Orleans. Finally, they tied up at an island in the river for an overnight stop, but the unstable land mass sank during the night. Tiger likely saved the boat from destruction by alerting them to oncoming tremors.

On December 22, just three days later, they encountered the British naturalist John Bradbury on a boat at the mouth of the St. Francis River; he told them that the town of Big Prairie was gone. Then, on December 30, they docked at Natchez, Mississippi, and celebrated the first marriage aboard a steamboat on December 31, when the steamboat engineer married Lydia's maid. They arrived at New Orleans ten days later on January 10, 1812, their destination reached after traveling 1,900 miles from Pittsburgh on the first steamboat to travel the western waters during what would be considered the most bizarre float trip ever.

OREGON COUNTY: GRAND GULF STATE PARK, MISSOURI GRAND CANYON

Not only does the Missouri Ozarks have streams and rivers and lakes located in picturesque farmland composed of rolling hills and forested valleys, but it also has Missouri's version of the Grand Canyon.

Located in Koshkonong (Oregon County), the Grand Gulf State Park spans 322 acres that a visitor won't soon forget. The park is six miles west of Thayer in the extreme south of the state. In fact, if you went any farther south, you'd be in Arkansas.

This breathtaking natural wonder is the remains of a dolomite cave system that collapsed thousands of years ago. It has been noted as the most spectacular collapsed cave system in the Ozarks. The Grand Gulf stretches for nearly a mile between soaring 130-foot-high limestone walls. Visitors can view the gulf from hiking trails or from the canyon floor, where they can walk 75 feet beneath the natural rock bridge, which spans 250 feet. Because the area is heavily wooded, some visitors prefer to visit the canyon during fall or winter, when leaves have fallen. The trail has scenic overlooks with stairs in places, and interpretive signs detail information about the gulf, yet there's no official trail leading to the canyon floor, according to Area Wide News and Missouri State Parks.

114

Grand Gulf State Park, known as the "Missouri Grand Canyon," is the most spectacular collapsed dolomite cave in the Ozarks. *Courtesy of Wikimedia Commons, Kbh3rd.*

Missouri Ozarks Legends & Lore

Reynolds County, Middle Brook: Johnson's Shut-Ins

148 Taum Sauk Trail, Middle Brook, MO 63656

Anyone who pines to swim among billion-year-old rocks (and who doesn't?) should head to Johnson's Shut-Ins State Park to experience the astounding shut-ins that were formed over hundreds of millions of years by unremitting forces of nature.

Johnson's Shut-Ins State Park covers 8,781 acres on the East Fork Black River. The unique shut-ins consist of igneous rock comprising molten rock, magma and other volcanic materials. Pink granites and blue-gray rhyolites were formed from volcanic activity. Igneous granite rock formed from magma that cooled below the earth's surface and was exposed later by erosion. Igneous rhyolite rock formed from magma and volcanic ash and debris flows that spewed out onto the surface and then cooled. Above the park, the East Fork of the Black River flows through a broader valley formed in dolomite (sedimentary) bedrock. When the river hit the more resistant igneous rock, the valley narrowed to form steep-sided chutes, or shut-ins.

Johnson's Shut-Ins, where visitors can swim among billion-year-old rocks in rural Missouri's ancient St. Francois Mountains. *Courtesy of Wikimedia Commons, Kbh3rd.*

Chapter 14

ST. FRANCOIS THROUGH WARREN COUNTY

BONNE TERRE: THE MINE AT BONNE TERRE

185 Park Avenue, Bonne Terre, MO 63628

Bonne Terre Mine, one of the world's largest man-made caverns, is listed as one of America's top ten greatest adventures by *National Geographic*. Founded in 1860, this historic deep-earth lead mine was the world's largest producer of lead ore until it closed in 1962. It was added to the National Register of Historic Places in 1974.

Currently, boat and walking tours reveal its interior rooms that still house abandoned tools and cat walks. Two upper levels are included in the one-hour guided walking tour along old mule trails, circa 1860. Three lower levels form a one-billion-gallon, seventeen-mile-long lake that is illuminated under water by stadium lighting. Boat tours on the crystal-clear water offer views of abandoned shafts and equipment below the water's surface.

Incredibly, Bonne Terre Mine is home to the largest freshwater scuba diving venue in the world, making it one of the most unusual diving destinations anywhere. Its clear illuminated water provides divers visibility to navigate and see artifacts throughout the mine.

The Mine at Bonne Terre, circa 1860, is noted by National Geographic as one of the most unusual scuba diving destinations in the world. *Courtesy of The Mine at Bonne Terre.*

Missouri Ozarks Legends & Lore

Ste. Genevieve County

*The Mississippi River towns are comely, clean, well built,
and pleasing to the eye, and cheering to the spirit. The Mississippi Valley
is as reposeful as a dreamland, nothing worldly about it,
nothing to hang a fret or a worry upon.*
—*Mark Twain,* Life on the Mississippi

Cave Vineyard and Distillery

The Cave Vineyard, associated with Salpeter Cave, located in Ste. Genevieve, is a must-see county wine destination, especially during the peak of fall color. To my senses, the sight and smell of the woods, along with the sound of leaves moving in the wind, adds legs to the wine. But that's just the sentiment of a gypsy soul revisiting Ozark roots during a road trip at the peak of fall color.

This friendly, family-owned establishment extends an invitation to visit its Wine Cellar, to experience the tasting room on top of the cave by sampling

Cave Vineyard's barrel room, where visitors can relax and drink wine inside Salpeter Cave. *Courtesy of the Cave Winery and Distillery, Ste. Genevieve, Missouri.*

A short walk from Cave Vineyard's tasting room reveals the entrance to Salpeter Cave. *Author's collection.*

MISSOURI OZARKS LEGENDS & LORE

Strussione Wines made from grapes grown within sight of the tasting room. Your purchase of at least one bottle is your admission ticket to enter Salpeter Cave, just a scenic short walk from the tasting room. The ambient cave has lighting and bistro tables where visitors enjoy their wine and contemplate mysterious shadows cast on living limestone walls. They will even pack a picnic basket for you, or you can bring your own. If drinking wine in a cave is not your forte, check out the aboveground pavilion with views of the vineyard and rolling Ozark hills.

Bequette-Ribault House

The Bequette-Ribault House was built by Jean-Baptiste Bequette Sr. in 1808 and is listed in the National Register of Historic Places. The two-room house is most noted for its Norman truss and poteaux-en-terre construction, or "posts in the earth," a reference to its vertical logs built directly into the ground. Five such structures remain in the United States, and Ste. Genevieve is home to three of them. The Bequette-Ribault House is a medium-sized Creole house about thirty-six feet in length with two chimneys.

The Bequette-Ribault House, circa 1808, is a two-room structure of post-in-ground construction about thirty-six feet in length, and it is one of only five remaining structures like it in the country. *Courtesy of Ste. Genevieve Visitor's Center.*

121

Above: The Green Tree Tavern (circa 1790) has rare post-on-sill vertical log construction. *Author's collection.*

Left: Green Tree Tavern exterior wall showing mud and straw packed between vertical logs as insulation. *Author's collection.*

MISSOURI OZARKS LEGENDS & LORE

French Colonial architecture found in Ste. Genevieve is of the highest concentration of distinctive types in the country. Poteaux-sur-sol, or "post on sill," features vertical logs placed onto a horizontal sill of wood or stone. Prominent local examples of this and poteaux-en-terre include the Beauvais-Amoureux House, the Felix Vallé House State Historic Site, La Maison de Guibourd, the Delassus-Kern House, the Louis Bolduc House (itself listed separately as a National Historic Landmark) and Old Miller Switch train station, which was a vital part of history, providing supplies and rest on the Old Railroad.

Green Tree Tavern interior wall showing a ghost image of a former staircase. *Author's collection.*

The Green Tree Tavern is the oldest vertical log building in Ste. Genevieve. Officially dated to 1790, this poteaux-sur-sole construction was built by the French Canadian Nicolas Janis. This historic structure has been an inn, a tobacco store and the first Masonic Lodge in Missouri. It was added to the National Register of Historic Places in 2001.

Throughout its history, Ste. Genevieve was notably the capital of Spanish Louisiana and the capital of French Louisiana, during the late eighteenth century. It is the oldest settlement west of the Mississippi and the location of rare French Colonial buildings that survived the Civil War. Ste. Genevieve Historic District encompasses much of the built environment of Ste. Genevieve, Missouri. Within the boundaries of this small Midwest town, you'll find the Ste. Genevieve National Historical Park and a National Historic Landmark District. A brief history of the town follows.

1700s

In 1750, Ste. Genevieve was established by French colonists when the territory west of the Mississippi River was part of French Louisiana. Ste. Genevieve was the principal regional civic center, and when the area passed into Spanish control with the Treaty of Paris in 1763, it continued as such. In 1785, a Mississippi River flood severely damaged the original site of Ste.

123

MISSOURI OZARKS LEGENDS & LORE

Genevieve. Afterward, the city relocated to its present site on higher ground, which is also on the river but three miles north of the original site. The oldest surviving buildings in the city date to this period. The agricultural area just outside the city to the southeast is largely still laid out as it was in 1793, following traditional French Colonial lines.

1800s

By 1810, Americans had begun to arrive in Ste. Genevieve after the Louisiana Purchase and were followed by immigrant groups as the nineteenth century progressed. By the mid-nineteenth century, German Americans were making up the single largest population group in the city.

1900s

In 1904, the city became the western end of a railroad ferry that connected to Kellogg, Illinois. In 1960, a large area of the city, including fields along the Mississippi River, was designated a National Historic Landmark District for two reasons: historic French architecture and land-use patterns.

2000s

In 2002, a smaller area, specific to parts of the city that are historically important (1790–1950), was named separately to the National Register for its French Colonial architecture. In 2018, the National Park Service established Ste. Genevieve National Historical Park as a unit of the U.S. national park system, and Ste. Genevieve joined the park system on October 30, 2020. Geologists identified a new seismic zone stretching from St. Louis to Cape Girardeau along the Mississippi River and called it the Ste. Genevieve Seismic Zone. Their research indicates that the zone is capable of producing moderate earthquakes every few decades and has the potential to produce a major earthquake every two to four thousand years.

124

SHANNON COUNTY: OZARK NATIONAL SCENIC RIVERWAYS

Located in Shannon County deep in the heart of the Ozark Salem Plateau, the Ozark National Scenic Riverways comprises eighty thousand acres designated for recreational use and is home to abundant animal and plant species.

The park was created to protect the Current and Jacks Fork Rivers. But its creation was not without problems. A political contest ensued for control of river recreational development between two federal agencies: the National Park Service (NPS) and the National Forest Service. Local residents opposed NPS plans because they included eminent domain acquisition of private property. Both agencies presented rival bills to Congress, and in 1964, the NPS plan was selected; the riverways area was formally dedicated in 1971. The Big Spring Historic District in Carter County was listed in the National Register of Historic Places by 1981.

The headwaters of the Current River begin at the confluence of Pigeon Creek and Montauk Springs in Montauk State Park. The park is located mostly in Shannon County but extends into Carter, Dent and Texas Counties. Communities surrounding the Ozark National Scenic Riverways include Eminence, Licking, Salem, Van Buren, Ellington, Bunker and Mountain View.

The park service promotes the Current River as one of the best float streams in the Midwest, in part due to the contributions of some of the nation's largest springs, such as Welch, Cave, Pulltite, Round, Fire Hydrant, Ebb and Flow, Blue, Big and Gravel Springs. The park contains the largest concentration of first-magnitude springs, defined as having average flow of more than one hundred cubic feet in dolomite rock in the United States. Now, that's quite a long list of natural springs. Given this, it's no surprise that feral horses and herds of elk that were introduced on nearby state land are prospering and expected to grow in numbers.

About 1.3 million people visit the scenic riverways annually for outdoor recreation that centers on the water. Canoeing, kayaking and inflatable rafts and tubes are popular for river float trips; however, motorized johnboats are allowed on the water as well. Visitors can also enjoy horseback riding, hunting, fishing, camping, hiking, birdwatching, sightseeing and nature photography. The riverways park features many caves, such as Round Spring Caverns, and other notable caves like Devils Well and Jam-Up Cave.

The Ozark Trail crosses the park at Rocky Falls and again at the Current River on Highway 106 at the town of Powder Mill. Now, these two points, in my opinion, are locations where paranormal activity is likely to occur. They sit at the crossroads, which have their own unique energy, and that energy is magnified by moving water. Add that to dolomite and limestone caves and you have the recipe for strange goings on there in the wilderness on the 37th parallel. Be sure to pack a camera and extra batteries!

WARREN COUNTY:
MARTHASVILLE AND THE EMMAUS HOME

Warren County, located in eastern Missouri, was organized in 1833 and named after General Joseph Warren, who died during the Revolutionary War in the Battle of Bunker Hill. Its scenic rolling hills are known as the "Missouri Weinstrasse," with its many vineyards along hilly and curvy Highway 94, which spans Marthasville to St. Charles County. Likewise, Warren County is part of the "Missouri Rhineland," with award-winning wineries along both sides of the Missouri River.

I chose Marthasville's Emmaus Home to include in this narrative because of its stunning landscape setting and outstanding German architecture of the historic home. Stories I have to share are of my own personal experiences, plus accounts of several hauntings as witnessed by workers at the home.

The historic Emmaus Home speaks to a time when buildings were constructed to last forever, seemingly. In design, it's like a fortress made of limestone blocks. The architect is said to be Isaac L. Taylor, as his prolific style is repeated in many downtown St. Louis buildings. Taylor also designed the famous haunted 1896 Crescent Hotel in Eureka Springs, Arkansas.

The Emmaus Home sits back off Missouri County Road D. It is separated from the blacktop road by a clearing of several acres surrounded by thick woods of deciduous trees—a sight to behold when fall color is at its peak. A narrow stone bridge spanning a small creek transitions the visitor from the county road onto the grounds and a winding drive leading to the entry of the three-story limestone building.

Constructed by thousands of German artisan craftsmen who immigrated here beginning in the 1830s, the campus consisting of five buildings and was completed in 1859. It was originally a seminary for the German Evangelical Church in Missouri, which operated at this site until 1883, when the seminary moved to St. Louis and became Eden Seminary.

From 1893 until about 2015, the Marthasville campus operated as the Emmaus Asylum for Epileptics and Feeble Minded. By 1928, the campus

The former Emmaus Asylum for Epileptics and Feeble Minded will be included in a $100 million revitalization of area wineries as a national destination. *Author's collection.*

had expanded to a total of eight buildings, including a chapel. A fire in 1930 claimed the College Building, leaving four of the original five buildings: the Farm House, Bake Oven, Friedensbote ("Messenger of Peace") Publishing House and the Dormitory. The integrity of the existing buildings remains strong to this day, proving the tenacity of Missouri's earliest German emigrant craftsmen. The buildings have few modifications from the original construction well over 150 years ago.

The home was listed for sale in 2016, 2017, 2018 and 2019 for $6 million. In October 2020, it sold at auction, where it was listed on Places in Peril in the hopes of going for $3 million. Currently, it is listed for sale at $849,000 but is valued at more than $4 million. (Places in Peril, instituted as a media campaign in 2000, calls attention to endangered statewide historic resources that are threatened by deterioration, lack of maintenance, insufficient funds, imminent demolition and/or inappropriate development. By publicizing these places, it hopes to build support toward each property's eventual preservation. Properties are nominated by concerned individuals and then approved by volunteer preservation professionals.)

My husband's family built a house just up the road from the Emmaus Home during the 1960s. The mid-century split-level is built right into the limestone hillside, an innovation for its time. I had the pleasure of living there in 1971, and it was an experience of enormous consequence for this city girl. Never before had I witnessed a night sky without city lights—a black velvet sky with a blanket of stars from horizon to horizon.

Grandmother Grace Sollis Carroll worked at the Emmaus Home as a cook. On the days she worked, she'd stay overnight in rotations of three or four days. There were many times I'd drive her to work or bring her back home; I was always in awe of the essence of the Emmaus Home.

From Highway D, I'd turn left onto the property and then cross the narrow one-lane rock bridge, where one of the male residents was always on the bridge stacking rocks on its parapet wall. Legend has it that he had been a bridge builder who fell while working and sustained a debilitating brain injury. Whether the story is true, it has been repeated time and again among the locals.

The majestic property never felt spooky to me. Well, except when driving down there in pitch dark under the black sky and looking for UFOs, but you can chalk that up to a skittish city girl dependent on streetlights and traffic signals. Frankly, seeing a deer in the wild would freak me out. But the isolated home was easy and quiet, remote yet peaceful, and to me it felt like the refuge it was intended to be.

Emmaus Home Haunts

However, others have documented their claims that Emmaus is haunted on the Missouri Ghosts/Emmaus Home Stories website. Grandmother Grace Carroll never spoke of experiences there because, frankly, she was prudent in more ways than one.

Another woman who worked there for four years claims to have experienced a lot of paranormal activity; she also claims to not be afraid of ghosts and embraces spectral encounters. In fact, she'd like to be a ghost hunter. Here are a few examples.

During a major snowstorm that hit Marthasville one winter, the twisty and hilly Ozark country roads would be treacherous, so an employee and her boss stayed at the home and teamed up to work all evening. They made a series of bed checks throughout the night on the floor that housed profoundly disabled men. Little could they have known that they'd encounter a ghostly prankster.

Starting at one end of a hall, they worked their way around a series of patients' rooms that contained lockers with doors that got stuck easily. You had to pull hard on those old locker doors to get them open. She encountered a door standing open that she was certain she'd closed earlier that evening. She closed it again and went on with her duties. On the second and third rounds of bed checks, the same locker door was found standing open once and again.

She yelled, "Stop opening the doors. This is getting irritating." It didn't happen again.

When working the night shift, another employee heard footsteps and saw a blue mist walk by her station. Rather than being startled, she was happy to have seen a ghost.

An Emmaus Home employee has heard and seen things in several locations. A picture she took one night of the abandoned and dilapidated old house shows a woman looking back at her from a window. She cannot explain the photo or the feeling that someone is watching her, but it gives her chills.

Likewise, of the various free-standing buildings located on the Emmaus campus, the Merten Building has a creepy vibe. The old building has not been used for some time, and inside there is a strong presence that even a skeptic of paranormal goings-on will sense.

Update: Around the time this book was about to be published, the Emmaus Home found a buyer! The Hoffmann Family of Companies is planning to purchase fifty acres of Emmaus Home in Marthasville that will include nearly all the buildings on the property.

David Hoffmann and his wife, Jerri, are natives of Washington, Missouri, a town just across the Missouri River from Marthasville. They are real estate investors who specialize in revitalization, having already revived downtown Naples, Florida; Winnetka, Illinois; and Avon, Colorado. Now they are turning their attention to their roots and the quaint towns of Augusta and Marthasville, Missouri.

Their plan to develop a $100 million winery would make Augusta a national destination rivaling that of Napa and Sonoma Valley. The area will be renamed Martha's Vineyard and Winery, and there are plans for a resort hotel and bus system connecting Marthasville to Augusta. Plans include a luxury yacht that will transport visitors on the Missouri River from Marthasville to downtown Augusta. This is good news indeed!

Chapter 15

ST. LOUIS CITY

The first time I saw St. Louis, I could have bought it for six million dollars, and it was the mistake of my life that I did not do it.
—*Mark Twain,* Life on the Mississippi

St. Louis has astounding historic neighborhoods defined by European-style buildings. I strongly urge anyone interested in delving into the historic soul of this city to explore by way of home tours in the following three historic neighborhoods. Alphabetically, they are Benton Park's October fall home tour, Lafayette Square's spring and holiday home tours in June and December and Soulard's annual holiday parlor tour in December.

St. Louis Crossroads Energy

Not only is St. Louis a powerful natural crossroads, but the ground also contains earth elements that support paranormal activity: abundant moving water, iron and limestone quartz crystal. People have been drawn here since prehistoric times and have left proof of their time here in the form of artifacts found in caves and in the ground.

Moving Water—Three rivers become one where the Illinois and Missouri Rivers merge with the Mississippi River north of the Gateway Arch. In addition, the Meramec River empties into the Mississippi to the southwest of St. Louis. This conduit channels universal energy (chi) as the life-sustaining Mississippi River moves water more than 2,300 miles before flowing into the Gulf of Mexico.

IRON—Trains travel parallel to the river along iron tracks where burial mounds of an extinct mound culture once dominated the landscape. Like energy channeled through moving water, the element of iron channels energy through the railroad tracks that dissect the landscape. Iron also appears in locally crafted red brick, used in buildings in the city.

LIMESTONE—An intricate network of limestone caves culminates in the living urban cave known as Cherokee Cave, located beneath Benton Park. Most, if not all, buildings in Soulard are built on foundations crafted from limestone blocks.

The Gateway Arch

Finnish American architect Eero Saarinen (1910-1961) took an abstract concept and created one of the most iconic monuments in the world: the St. Louis Arch. From its concept to the finished design, it took an astonishing span of three decades. Mr. Saarinen died in 1961 and did not see the completion of the St. Louis Arch in 1965. It's notable that he also designed the St. Louis Lambert Airport terminal, circa 1933, which is defined by its rows of arched windows and is topped off by an impressive arched copper roof.

The National Park Service's 1933 original call for design was for a memorial that would transcend spiritual and aesthetic values and symbolize American culture and civilization. It wanted a central feature in the form of a single shaft, building or arch. Civic leaders pushed for a spiritual public space, a memorial to the frontier and accomplishment of expansion. They received all of this and much more.

In 1940, seven years after the National Park Service announced its plan for a national monument, acreage along the Mississippi Riverfront was acquired and cleared for the memorial.

In February 1948, of the 172 design submissions, Eero Saarinen's design was chosen unanimously by the judging panel, with some noting that Saarinen's concept was relevant and beautiful, an inspired abstract form rich in symbolism. In 1959, eleven years later, they broke ground to begin construction for the Arch. On February 12, 1963, construction began, and on October 28, 1965, the Arch was completed.

The Arch design concept is based on an inverted catenary curve, a free-hanging chain bending under its own weight. The dip is created by tension

MISSOURI OZARKS LEGENDS & LORE

The Gateway Arch at the Mississippi River, an inverted catenary curve designed by Aero Saarinen, is cited as one of the most iconic monuments in the world. *Courtesy of Wikimedia Commons, Tarthur4469.*

from each end and is supported entirely by compression from its own weight, with no strain on the structure. The width and height of the Arch are identical at 630 feet. Each of the legs is an equilateral triangle of 54 feet at the base, narrowing to 17 feet where the two join at the top.

LEGEND: MARK TWAIN'S PREMONITION DREAM

I came in with Halley's Comet in 1835. It is coming again next year, and I expect to go out with it. The Almighty has said, no doubt, "Now there are these two unaccountable freaks; they came in together, they must go out together."
—*Mark Twain 1909*

Mark Twain, the Missouri native and consummate cave explorer, had a lifelong interest in paranormal goings-on, especially the topics of telepathy and clairvoyance. In fact, he was born in 1835 during the presence of Halley's Comet and correctly predicted that he'd leave this earth when it returned in 1910.

132

Missouri Ozarks Legends & Lore

In 1858, Samuel Clemens was employed on the steamboat *Pennsylvania*. At just twenty-three, he was a steersman and had arranged for his twenty-year-old brother, Henry, to work with him on the same ship.

In late spring or early summer that year, the *Pennsylvania* docked at St. Louis, where Twain's older sister lived. That night, he stayed with his sister and experienced a lucid nightmare. In the dream, Twain stood in a parlor where two chairs supported a metallic coffin. In the coffin lay Henry, dressed in one of Twain's own suits. A bouquet of white flowers with a single crimson bloom was placed on his chest.

Twain awoke believing that Henry had died, not realizing it was a dream. Before going to view his brother's corpse, he went for an early morning walk to gather his thoughts. In the morning air, Twain realized that he had dreamed the scene. He raced back to the house and rushed into the sitting room to discover there was no coffin. He was able to put the dream behind him once the *Pennsylvania* set sail to New Orleans.

Because of friction with the soon-to-be-fired pilot of the *Pennsylvania*, and in order to prevent more trouble, Twain volunteered to steer the *A. T. Lacey* instead, a boat that had left two days after Henry left on the *Pennsylvania*. On June 13, 1858, the *Pennsylvania*'s boilers exploded when the steamboat was south of Memphis, sinking the ship and killing 250 of the 500 passengers and crew outright. Henry was on that boat at the time of the explosion and was blown into the river by the blast. He swam back to the ship to rescue others, even though he'd been fatally injured. His lungs were damaged by inhaling steam and his skin scalded.

With his brother at his side, Henry lingered a full week and died in his sleep on June 20, 1858. As a houseguest in Memphis, grief paired with exhaustion left Twain in a kind of trance until he finally collapsed into deep sleep. Later, he arose and discovered a sitting room in the house where he was staying. Inside the room were two chairs supporting a metal coffin. Twain was standing looking at his young brother's corpse when an elderly woman placed a bouquet of flowers on Henry's chest, all white flowers but for one crimson bloom in the center (as documented on the Anomaly Info website). Is it possible that the trinity of earth elements present at St. Louis could have created an environment that delivered to Samuel Clemens a premonition dream?

133

MISSOURI OZARKS LEGENDS & LORE

NEIGHBORHOOD SITES

Historic Benton Park, circa 1866

Listed in the National Register of Historic Places in 1985 and the City Historic District in 2006, historic Benton Park picks up where Soulard (circa 1790) leaves off. These sister neighborhoods share proximity to the Mississippi River, rich history, folklore and urban legend, and Benton Park is underscored by a network of caves leading to Cherokee and English Caves, located below Lemp Brewery on Arsenal Street. Like Soulard and Lafayette Square, Benton Park lies within the 37th parallel band.

Benton Park's awe-inspiring architecture showcases Queen Ann, Romanesque and Classical Revival styles crafted by St. Louis builders and masons and contractors of German descent. Terra-cotta, pressed brick, stamped metal and cast-iron materials detail buildings of all sizes ranging from studios to mansions.

Benton Park has more standalone buildings than Soulard's block after block of rowhouses because caves below Benton Park can't support the weight associated with rowhouses. An assortment of one-to-three-story buildings stand side by side in Benton Park, divided by narrow gangways measuring about three feet wide.

City Cemetery

During 1836, the City of St. Louis began selling the Common Fields, a large tract of undeveloped pastureland outside the western boundary of the city limits at Eighteenth Street. Ten acres were originally set aside for the City Cemetery at the time of the land sale and laid out for cemetery purposes in 1842. City Cemetery was heavily utilized for the victims of the 1849 cholera epidemic, which killed 10 percent of the city's population. In 1865, bodies were exhumed and relocated to the quarantine burial grounds on Arsenal Island, located in the middle of the Mississippi River. The original cemetery was the first site of what is now Benton Park's city park and playground, located at Jefferson and Arsenal Streets—my childhood playground. Gruesome.

Gus' Pretzel Factory

Gus' Pretzels, a landmark pretzel factory located at 1820 Arsenal Street in the Benton Park neighborhood, has been operating since 1920, when it was first opened by Frank Ramperger. The third-generation family business is located near the Anheuser-Busch brewery. Fresh pretzels are characteristic of the German American culture and community that were prominent in St. Louis, the offspring of German breweries that dominated the city before Prohibition.

When I was a child growing up in Benton Park, Gus' featured an exterior walk-up window where customers lined up to buy pretzels fresh out of the oven. An enclosed walk-up counter has replaced the exterior walk-up window, and an added plus is that now you can get containers of Ted Drewes frozen custard at the counter. It's heaven on Arsenal Street. Street vendors sold pretzels (from the 1930s to the 1960s) seemingly on every major intersection in the area, where we'd hustle for coins to pay for our pretzels before the traffic signal changed to green. Gus' Pretzels is a stone's throw from the Lemp Mansion.

Venice Café

Venice Café's legend is about as funky as the café itself, according to Atlas Obscura. As the lore goes, owner Jeff Lockheed purchased the building at 1903 Pestalozzi back in 1978, giving credence to the idea that by doing what you love, happiness will follow. After letting friends hang around for nearly a decade, Lockheed converted his home into a café, applied for a liquor license and adopted a new business model: "Booze and Beauty for Cash."

The "beauty" that Venice Café alludes to is a riot of colorful mosaics, a folk art vibe found inside the café and extending to the outdoor courtyard garden seating. The creative vibe is both vivid and frenetic and would have been comfortable in the psychedelic era. For some, that spells nostalgia—for others, it spells magic.

Exterior walls are works of art, curated with ashtrays and lighters, action figures and anything else that came too close on a windy St. Louis day. The outdoor garden sports a bar that is crafted from the front end of a boat, where the bartender mixes cocktails from behind the steering wheel. Inside, every visible surface is covered with mosaics and quirky collages that achieve the ambiance of a fantasy set design. Its lighting blends more

MISSOURI OZARKS LEGENDS & LORE

than twenty different light fixtures in primary red, yellow and blue, with splashes of green—as if a fractured prism is responsible for refracting light every which way.

Meandering downstairs on the staircase located below a sign that reads "Shitters," you'll encounter an ATM and a fish tank, as well as a renewed expanse of mosaics that spill into two bathrooms before surrounding the porcelain thrones.

Meandering upstairs to the Explorer's Lounge, which opens on Friday and Saturday nights, prepare to meet Mr. Waylon Slithers, a king snake. Mr. Slithers greets guests from his tank behind the bar—that is, if he's not sleeping in his turtle shell. Taxidermy and artwork appropriately decorate the Explorer's Lounge. Fittingly, the lounge's bathroom goes by the title "The Blue Hole" and is filled with curiosities that span the animal kingdom, from ceramic lions to monkey statues that hold toilet paper to more mosaics.

Turtles Myrtle and Shemmy reside in an adjacent pond. A nearby sign reads: "Please don't throw pennies in the pond. You'll hurt the shell babies and your dumb wish will never come true."

Lemp Mansion

Within walking distance of our Wisconsin flat, a circa 1868 haunted old mansion remains standing to this day. It lies within the Benton Park National Historic District and the Cherokee-Lemp Local Historic District and is designated as a St. Louis City Landmark. It also lies near the Soulard and Lafayette Square National Historic Districts. My family's proximity to a mansion does not indicate that we were people of wealth. The opposite is true. Our section of the Benton Park neighborhood comprised brownstone multi-family flats originally built to house brewery workers and their families. My young parents would sometimes drive by the old mansion just for the thrill of being scared. Rampant urban legend presented the mansion as an insane asylum, and we kids were on the prowl for wild-eyed patients in straitjackets.

Well, it happens that the old mansion is a well-known haunt that is often featured on ghost hunter documentaries. It is the notorious acclaimed Lemp Mansion, currently a restaurant with a bed-and-breakfast option for the brave and curious. The restaurant serves the best food I've ever had in a haunted mansion. The Sunday menu is worth raving over: home-

136

Benton Park's Lemp Mansion (circa 1868), listed in National Register of Historic Places, was built over a limestone cave and is documented as one of the most haunted places in the country. *Courtesy of Wikimedia Commons.*

style dishes featuring southern down-home panache, delivered in family-style serving bowls. No doubt this southern-style culinary chef-d'oeuvre dished up in an Italianate haunted mansion requires a reservation ahead of time—never mind that the hostess is the personable medium featured on the Lemp Mansion *Ghost Hunters* episode or that Lemp family-style offerings on Sunday are worthy of an overnight Amtrak from Houston.

Designed by Jacob Feikert, the Italianate Lemp Mansion, located in the St. Louis section of Benton Park, was built in 1868 for William J. Lemp and his family. The house features a spiral staircase leading down to the living urban Cherokee Cave, where the family had built not only a swimming pool but also a theater.

The mansion was in such serious decline that in about 1950 the interior space was divided up and converted into a boardinghouse. Over the next decade, it lost much of its ornate architectural artifacts and nearly met the wrecking ball in the 1960s, when construction of the I-55 corridor brought about destruction to Soulard and Benton Park. Much of Lemp Mansion's grounds and one of the carriage houses were destroyed when the interstate corridor plowed through the old neighborhoods.

MISSOURI OZARKS LEGENDS & LORE

One fascinating unintended consequence of tearing down those old buildings is this: where one building that was connected to another is taken down, it leaves an impression on the remaining newly exposed wall. The impression is the shape of the demolished building and is referred to as an architectural ghost.

The Lemp Mansion, which *LIFE* magazine listed in 1980 as one of the ten most haunted places in America, is the site of three suicides by Lemp family members after the death of son Frederick Lemp, and it is said to be haunted by members of the Lemp family. Some have concluded that the eeriest room in Lemp Mansion is the tower room on the north side, where the windows are located near the ceiling. The Lemp's child, who had Down syndrome and whose birth was never officially documented, was kept there in isolation until his death at age sixteen. He's allegedly entombed in the Lemp Mausoleum, without a name.

The infamous history and haunts of the Lemp Mansion captured the interest of ghost hunters. The story has been featured time and again in the media:

- On December 29, 2009, the mansion was investigated by the Discovery Channel program *If Walls Could Talk*.
- On September 29, 2010, an investigation by the Atlantic Paranormal Society was featured on *Ghost Hunters*.
- In 2011, caves below the mansion and brewery were featured on the show *Off Limits*, episode 1.1, showing exterior shots of the mansion.
- On October 13, 2013, the mansion was featured on the Travel Channel's *Most Terrifying Places in America*.
- On October 18, 2014, the mansion was featured on the Travel Channel's *Ghost Adventures*, episode 10; included were the mansion, the brewery and Cherokee Cave System.
- In 2014, the investigation group Kindred Moon Paranormal teamed up with Shannon Sylvia from the TV shows *Paranormal State* and *Ghost Hunters International* to investigate the infamous haunted Lemp Mansion in St. Louis, Missouri, on Halloween night.
- On July 23, 2016, the *History Goes Bump* podcast debuted "The Lemp Mansion" (episode 38).
- In October 2016, the mansion was featured on Syfy Channel's *Paranormal Witness* series, "The Hotel" (renamed "Locke Mansion Hotel" in the episode).

MISSOURI OZARKS LEGENDS & LORE

Additionally, there are quite a few podcasts and YouTube features. If you appreciate campy amateur videos, it's like hitting the jackpot. Nevertheless, they are out there for any interested party willing to sort it out. Also, see Kindred-Moon Paranormal for a Lemp Mansion investigation.

Historic Lafayette Square, circa 1836

Just three blocks south of downtown and the Gateway Arch lies St. Louis's oldest historic district. This reclaimed urban community is now a designated National Historic District.

A stroll through Lafayette Square reveals restored 150-year-old Victorian mansions in French Second Empire and Federalist architectural styles. *Better Homes and Gardens* recognized this designated National Historic District as one of the nation's prettiest painted places. And it's no wonder, with the two- and three-story painted ladies that feature bright yellow doors trimmed

Lafayette Square is St. Louis's oldest historic district. *Better Homes and Gardens* recognized this designated National Historic District as one of the nation's prettiest painted places in 2012. *Courtesy of flickr.com, stevenm.*

139

in aqua blue and brown. Positioned next to salmon and turquoise, they define their neighbors. Lime green and purple façades complement ornate moldings painted light blue in yet another astounding building.

The thirty-acre Lafayette Park centrally anchors the neighborhood. Dedicated in 1851, Lafayette Park is noted as the oldest urban park west of the Mississippi River. Additionally, its original iron and stone fence (circa 1869) borders the park. Lush greenery and historic bridges augment a circa 1896 music pavilion.

In addition to the private residences surrounding the park, the trendy and hip area houses two craft breweries, specialty shops, coffee shops and one-of-a-kind bistros and restaurants. Yoga, art studios, shops for wine and chocolate and rooftop bars abound. Three bed-and-breakfast inns featuring twelve-foot carved entry doors, garden courtyards, canopy beds and champagne breakfasts await visitors year-round.

Historic Soulard, circa 1790

One year in particular, my mother gained popularity on the Soulard shuttle tour bus by telling other riders about her experiences growing up in Soulard. Frankly, she was inherently the perfect storm of an extroverted personality with an outrageous sense of humor. Before we'd reached the next stop, this people magnet received two rounds of applause and one standing ovation on the bus.

My parents began their time together in a Soulard furnished flat at 315 Russell Boulevard. The flat, now demolished, was the embodiment of paranormal elements: a location three blocks from the Mississippi River and near the railroad tracks, a limestone block foundation and soaring walls crafted from red clay bricks. It's no surprise the flat was haunted! A beautiful blond ghost wearing a tailored red dress made midnight visits to my newlywed parents. Each night, she appeared one step closer than the night before. They moved out on the fifth day, like fugitives on the lam.

Come with me now as we time-travel into the past of historic Soulard, a Missouri neighborhood listed in the National Register of Historic Places. My birthplace:

"You belong here," Soulard whispers across time and space, spanning centuries and thousands of miles. "Come and walk along my red brick sidewalks and I'll show you magic amid shadows cast by historic rowhouses. Listen for lingering jangles of horse-drawn

Missouri Ozarks Legends & Lore

carriages over cobblestone streets. Discover my architectural ghosts and be charmed by phantom echoes from bell towers that once were and are no more. Encounter my mysteries and peek into the lives of those who lived and loved here, but remember to tread lightly among resident ghosts."

At the west bank of the Mississippi River, Soulard's location falls between the 36th and 38th parallels, otherwise known as the Paranormal Highway. Four distinct seasons cycle through Tornado Alley at St. Louis, where opposing weather fronts often collide to create white-knuckle storms. The New Madrid fault line runs through here, as if to emphasize an edgy vibe trailing the 1811–12 New Madrid earthquakes, the worst in recorded history. This blend of location and earth elements sets the stage for a perfect storm of unseen forces expressed through folklore and urban legend. Many a good ghost story involves the presence of moving water; the element of iron and geology comprising quartz crystal in limestone. It's a trinity of paranormal magnets, and Soulard has them all in abundance.

Soulard Farmers' Market (formed circa 1790; 1910 photograph) is listed in the National Register of Historic Places and located in the oldest walking neighborhood west of the Mississippi River. *Courtesy of mohistory.org, William G. Swekosky.*

MISSOURI OZARKS LEGENDS & LORE

CULTURAL HISTORY

Soulard's cultural history spans centuries, beginning with an extinct prehistoric mound culture and then continuing with eighteenth-century French explorers and settlers before moving into the nineteenth-century era of Bohemian immigrants. Later, twentieth-century hippies and yuppie rehabbers breathed life back into Soulard when neglect and poverty pushed it to the brink of ruin. By the twenty-first century, Soulard had transformed to a hot spot of trendy lifestyles. Mardi Gras and holiday home tours bring tens of thousands into its fold each year. Historically, it's been a self-contained blue-collar community driven by river trade, industry and German breweries. Schools and churches, restaurants and bars, merchants and a circa 1790 farmers' market—all are the lifeblood of this oldest walking neighborhood west of the Mississippi.

Boom-and-bust cycles move through Soulard like footprints in sands of time. Its evolution began when a prehistoric mound culture created a landscape of copious burial mounds. Before 1800, settlers had leveled burial mounds and divided fertile land into grid-plotted farmland and orchards. All this before the 1804 Lewis and Clark Expedition mapped territory in tandem with the Louisiana Purchase.

By 1840, skilled French and German immigrants had transformed this 384-acre landscape into European styled architecture that stands unchanged today. After 1840, an influx of Bohemian and artisan immigrants called it home. At my 1953 birth, Soulard was an urban slum populated by proud, working poor people. My people. I'm second-generation born in Soulard, sixth-generation Missouri native.

ARCHITECTURE

A mix of Federal, Transitional Federal, Italianate and Second Empire architectural styles grace Soulard's cityscape. Designated as a historic district in 1972, Soulard's rowhouses were completed before the advent of indoor plumbing or electricity. Brick paved alleyways led to horse-and-buggy carriage houses. Fire pits where trash was burned sat side by side with ubiquitous outhouses lining alleyways. All of this remained unchanged well into the twentieth century.

The '60s era of urban flight to St. Louis suburbs weakened Soulard, and although its architecture appeared as it did centuries ago, many buildings

142

stood abandoned. Mid-twentieth-century demolition took down nineteenth-century buildings in the name of progress to construct the interstate highway that runs through Soulard's western border. A path of historic structures met the wrecking ball when the interstate trough altered the landscape and divided the sister neighborhoods of Soulard and Benton Park.

Chapter 16

THE MISSOURI DALTONS

There is a charm about the forbidden that makes it unspeakably desirable.
—*Mark Twain*

In my Missouri Dalton family, the legend of our connection to the outlaws was handed down through the generations, yet details of our heritage path had been lost to time. Twain understood the charm of the forbidden, and for me that translated to proving that I had an ancestral connection to history's iconic Wild West outlaws.

I began researching Dalton genealogy in the late 1990s, well before genealogy search engines were available. I spent weeks at Houston's Clayton Genealogy Library, paging through microfiche for any morsel of information as a bumbling neophyte genealogist. Confusion resulted when identical names were used over and again in generations. For example, I found three James Lewis Daltons and several Adeline Daltons—all of the same era and related to one another. I incorrectly concluded that Adeline Lee Younger Dalton was my direct ancestor. What I know now is that she is a fourth-great-aunt, not a fifth-great-grandmother in the lineage.

What most surprised me about the Daltons is Adeline's story. She is a puzzle, and I felt compelled to assemble the pieces of this fascinating woman whose remarkable life story is overshadowed by her notorious outlaw sons.

I proceeded by obtaining official documents as my only source of viable information: state documents such as birth and death certificates or federal records such as census or military records. For example, my mother's birth

MISSOURI OZARKS LEGENDS & LORE

certificate shows her father as David Franklin Dalton (1906–1967), my grandfather, who was born in Mine Lamotte, Missouri. His documents show William Thomas (1870–1929) as his father. And so on until completing the thread to James Lewis (1798–1826). Why James? Because he is the father of brothers James Lewis (born in 1826; father of the Dalton Gang) and Henry Milton Dalton, my direct ancestor. This is my path to the Wild West Daltons: James Lewis, 1798–1826; Henry Milton, 1821–1896; Thomas J., 1849–1920; William Thomas, 1870–1929; David Franklin, 1906–1967; and Gerry Dalton, 1938–2012, my mother.

Adeline Lee Younger Dalton and James Lewis Dalton were the parents of the infamous Dalton Outlaw Gang. One irony in the Dalton lore is this: Adeline is likely the parent who carried those outlaw genes! She was an aunt to members of the Younger Gang, meaning her Dalton children were first cousins to the Younger outlaws, who rode with Jesse James, the Daltons' rival. Before I tell you about the gang, I'd like to tell you more about Adeline and James Dalton.

JAMES LEWIS DALTON (1826–1890), the son of a man who shares the exact same name, was born on February 16 in Mount Sterling, Montgomery, Kentucky. He was a shiftless jack of all trades—sometime farmer, sometime Kansas City saloonkeeper and sometime horse fancier.

James served an even 365 days under General Zachary Taylor in the Mexican-American War as a fifer in Company I, Second Regiment, Kentucky Foot Volunteers. For clarity, a fifer is one who plays a fife, which is a high-pitched transverse flute used in military and marching bands. James also served as a Confederate soldier during the American Civil War.

James was a Kansas City saloonkeeper when he married Adeline Lee Younger on March 12, 1851, in Missouri. At twenty-six years old, he was ten years the senior of sixteen-year-old Adeline. Three years later, they lived on Adeline's inherited two hundred-plus acres of Jackson County, Missouri farmland.

Over the course of the following twenty-six years, fifteen children were born to James and Adeline, thirteen of whom survived to adulthood. They migrated to Coffeyville, Kansas, and then James and Adeline left Kansas in 1890 late in life, at ages sixty-four and fifty-four. They headed to Indian Territory with their possessions loaded onto an ox-drawn wagon. James returned to Coffeyville, leaving Adeline on her own to homestead in Indian Territory.

James proved to be a steadily unsuccessful man and an ill-tempered misanthrope later in life. Known in Coffeyville as "Old Man Dalton," James died on July 16, 1890, near Deering, Montgomery County, at age seventy.

145

MISSOURI OZARKS LEGENDS & LORE

ADELINE LEE YOUNGER DALTON (1835–1925), as portrayed in a vintage photograph, appears typical for the era. In Victorian fashion, a ribbon accents her lacy high collar. Coarse hair parts straight down the middle and gathers in the back. Thin lips, sloped shoulders, no frills, no smile, no glam. With a broad forehead, wide-set eyes and squarish chin, she looks a bit masculine.

Adeline's personality is somewhat of a mystery; however, the woman must have had moxie made of steel. She birthed fifteen babies on the western frontier before the advent of antibiotics and vaccines as we know them today. Thirteen survived to adulthood. My assumption is that she was determined and organized, perhaps a task master attracted to her opposite with James's shiftlessness.

Adeline was born in 1835 in Jackson County, Missouri, the western border near Independence and Kansas City. While this is not the Missouri Ozarks of the Springfield Plateau, formed by uplift, some geologists will refer to it as Ozarks defined by what is beneath the surface—that is, sedimentary bedrock that formed when the area was an inland sea but did not rise in elevation when uplift created the Ozarks signature rolling hills. Some call this a stretch of the Ozark definition, while others consider it to be credible.

No matter the elevation of Jackson County, Missouri, Adeline was the daughter of Colonel Charles Lee Younger (1779–1854) and granddaughter of army veteran Colonel Joshua Younger (1752–1834), who fought in the Revolutionary War under George Washington.

Adeline was born to Parmelia Dorcus Wilson (1815–1882), the daughter of Thomas and Jane (Loyd) Wilson. Parmelia was the slave woman of Colonel Charles Lee Younger and the mother of nine of his children. Although all of her children were born with the last name Wilson, they were given the option to use the last name Younger per Charles Lee Younger's will, but only after his death in pre–Civil War times.

COLONEL CHARLES LEE YOUNGER, Adeline's father, was a dichotomous individual. In contrast to the colonel's oil portrait, where he's all done up in red velvet fancy pants, his last will and testament portrays a complex man at the end of life. Now, before judging the colonel, consider the following narrative, which I find simultaneously appalling and amusing.

To his legitimate wife, Sarah Sullivan Younger (and seven children), he bequeathed the sum of one dollar. Besides his legacy, he'd already given them as much as he intended.

To Coleman Younger (a son), he willed half his Jackson County, Missouri farm, with the stipulation that Coleman purchase the other half at $25 per acre. The nominal 1850 price of Missouri farmland was $7.98 per acre.

Missouri Ozarks Legends & Lore

He bequeathed that after his death, which was prior to the Civil War, the slaves he named as his own biological children would assume the Younger name and be forever set free from slavery or bondage to any man. To Parmelia Wilson (Adeline's mother), he left 80 acres; to Adeline, he left 210 acres; and to three additional mulatto slave women who also bore his children, he parceled out the remainder of his substantial estate. To his two youngest mixed-race children, he provided means of protection and a proper college education in a free state.

It's no wonder why his legitimate wife not only contested his will but also had the colonel's body exhumed from land he had bequeathed to the slave women who birthed his children. Sarah Sullivan had the last word by exhuming and relocating his butt to Orient Cemetery, Harrisonville, Cass County, Missouri.

Adeline married James Lewis Dalton on March 12, 1851 (at age sixteen). Three years later, Colonel Charles Lee Younger died, and she inherited 210 acres of Jackson County, Missouri farmland. During the next twenty-six years (1852-78), Adeline birthed fifteen children; the last were twins, born when she was forty-three years old. They are: Charles Benjamin "Ben" Dalton (1852), Henry Coleman "Cole" Dalton (1853), Louis Kossuth Dalton (1855), Bea Elizabeth "Lelia" Dalton (1856), Littleton Lee "Lit" Dalton (1857), Franklin "Frank" Dalton (1859), Gratton Hanley "Grat" Dalton (1861), William Marion "Bill" Dalton (1863), Eva Dalton (1867), Robert Rennick "Bob" Dalton (1869), Emmett Dalton (1871), Leona Randolph Dalton (1875), Nancy "Nannie" Dalton Clute (1876), Simon Noel "Sam" Dalton (1879) and Hannah Adeline Dalton (1879).

Of the ten male children listed here, Frank Dalton was a U.S. marshal killed in the line of duty, Grat, Bob and Emmett (in birth order) became the infamous outlaws.

FRANKLIN (FRANK) DALTON (1859–1887) was a deputy marshal in Fort Smith, Arkansas. He was sixth of fifteen in birth order and a role model to his younger brothers, who became outlaws after his death. As the older brother to Grat, Bob and Emmett, Frank was the most stable of the Dalton brothers. He presented as well-grounded and mature, and by all accounts he kept the others in line. They respected and admired him.

Tall, lean and handsome, with a steely-eyed gaze of a man who had seen it all, Frank had the look of a hero you'd see on the cover of a dime novel. Frank allegedly wasn't afraid of anything. He dressed to perfection, with his tall boots polished like mirrors, and he wore a short, rounded hat with a narrow brim.

MISSOURI OZARKS LEGENDS & LORE

Frank was killed in the line of duty (at age twenty-eight) while tracking a horse thief in the Oklahoma Territory. When he confronted the suspect, a shootout erupted resulting in Frank and two outlaws being killed and his deputy being wounded.

GRATTON ('GRAT') HANLEY DALTON (1861–1892) was seventh of fifteen in birth order and the eldest of the outlaw brothers. From the time Grat was a young boy, he was always looking for a fight. According to Emmett's book, titled *When the Daltons Rode*, Grat's reputation was that of a slow-witted thug whose avocations were thumping other people, gambling and drinking copious amounts of liquor. He was described as having the heft of a bull calf and disposition of a baby rattlesnake.

Even so, Grat was a lawman early on who rode alongside his older brother Frank but turned to crime three years after Frank's death. When the Dalton brothers began dealing in horses, rumors spread like wildfire that they were stealing horses from all over the country. This is a poignant reminder of Mark Twain's quote: "A lie can travel half way around the world while the truth is putting on its shoes."

Emmett and Bob fled the country when Grat was arrested for selling stolen horses. Grat later joined Bob, Emmett and Bill in California, where they held up a Southern Pacific Railroad passenger train in the town of Alila on February 6, 1891, killing the train's engineer when he tried to escape. Although Bob and Emmett fled the scene, Grat and Bill were arrested for train robbery. Bill was acquitted at trial, but Grat was convicted and given a twenty-year sentence; however, he escaped custody.

There are two accounts of how Grat managed to escape. One of them has Grat breaking out of jail with two other men. The other is much more entertaining, claiming that Grat was being taken to prison by train, accompanied by two deputies. He was handcuffed to one of them but slipped the handcuff key out of the deputy's pocket when the lawman dozed off. He undid the cuffs and waited until the train reached the trestle bridge over the San Joaquin River. Then he jumped through the window into the river and swam away a free man.

WILLIAM (BILL) MARION DALTON (1866–1894) was the lookout and informant for the Dalton Gang. After Grat and Bob were killed in 1892 at Coffeyville, Bill Dalton formed another gang with Bill Doolin. Known as the Wild Bunch or the Dalton-Doolin Gang, their partnership was immortalized in the Eagles album *Desperado*. Also known as Mason Frakes Dalton, Bill was killed at the age of twenty-eight by a posse near Elk, Indian Territory, and is buried in an unmarked grave in the Blivens family plot, Turlock Memorial Park, Turlock, California.

148

Missouri Ozarks Legends & Lore

ROBERT (BOB) RENICK DALTON (1869–1892) was tenth of fifteen in birth order and was the leader of the outlaw gang. Known as a ladies' man, the handsome outlaw had a woman in every town, according to his younger brother Emmett, who idolized Bob to the point of hero worship. Bob favored his father. Tall and confident, Bob Dalton was intelligent, a natural-born leader and an excellent marksman. While riding as a posse man with Frank, Bob is said to have killed his first man at the age of nineteen. Like Grat and Emmett, Bob remained on the right side of the law for three years after Frank was killed but later took to stealing horses and illegally running liquor into Indian Territory. By 1892, he was robbing stagecoaches, trains and banks and was killed in the Coffeyville raid in October 1892 at the age of twenty-three.

EMMETT DALTON (1871–1937) was eleventh of fifteen in birth order and the youngest brother of the outlaw gang. A gentleman cowboy-outlaw, well liked and well-mannered yet fearless, Emmett loved excitement. He lacked the bloodthirsty bravado of the successful bandit, according to E.D. Nix, U.S. marshal at Guthrie in the 1890s, in his book, *Oklahombres*.

Like his brothers, Emmett began on the right side of the law, riding as posse man with Frank; then he turned to crime three years after Frank's death in the line of duty. Emmett is the only brother who survived the 1892 raid in Coffeyville. He served fourteen years in a Kansas prison before receiving a full pardon and then married and moved to California, where he became a successful writer, actor and real estate salesman. He died as a man of means in 1937 at the age of sixty-six.

When the new Oklahoma Territory was opened, the Daltons joined the land rush. Before James's 1890 death, he and Adeline Dalton chose the claim that was the southwest one-fourth of Section 11, in Township 17, north of Range 8 and west of the Indian Meridan in Oklahoma. This claim contained 160 acres, all bottomland, six miles northeast of the town of Kingfisher, Oklahoma. Times were hard in the new raw land. James Lewis Dalton, father of the clan, returned to Kansas to work in Coffeyville, while Adeline remained on the land (claim) with the children to prove it up. James Lewis Dalton died that same year, leaving the family on their own and leaving Adeline as head of household.

Adeline journeyed into Indian Territory and Cimarron Township, Oklahoma, where history records Adeline's race in "C and A" county openings. She secured 160 acres in Cooper Township, which is deeded solely to Adeline Younger Dalton.

To qualify under the Homestead Act of 1862, a homesteader had to be the head of a household or at least twenty-one years of age to claim a 160-

149

Missouri Ozarks Legends & Lore

acre parcel of land. Each homesteader had to live on the land, build a home, make improvements and farm for five years before they were eligible to prove up. A total filing fee of eighteen dollars was the only money required.

The Homestead Act of 1862 has been called one of the most important pieces of legislation in the history of the country. Signed into law by Abraham Lincoln after the secession of Southern states, this act turned over vast amounts of the public domain to private citizens. About 270 million acres, or 10 percent of the area of the United States, was claimed and settled under this act. Charles, Ben and Littleton Dalton took claims near Kingfisher; Henry Dalton participated in the Cherokee Strip land rush and took a claim near Enid, Oklahoma.

The gang formed in February 1891, put together by Bob, Grat and Emmett Dalton, along with George Newcomb, Charley Bryant and William McElhanie. They began robbing banks, stagecoaches and trains, while middle brother William (Bill) Dalton served as their spy and informant. Eventually, an attempt to rob two Coffeyville, Kansas banks simultaneously—in order to one-up Jesse James—led to their demise. Grat and Bob were killed, and Emmett was wounded and sentenced to life in prison. The Dalton Outlaw Gang's reign of terror was short-lived, beginning in February 1891 and ending in October 1892.

The gang, in a nutshell, was a small group of brothers from a large family. Their father was a shiftless but handsome jack of all trades, and their mother was born of the union of a wealthy plantation owner and his mulatto slave. Through their mother's father (Colonel Charles Lee Younger), the Dalton brothers were first cousins to the Younger Gang.

Kansas, the Sunflower State, is home to a slight portion of Ozarks that crosses state lines at the crossroads of Missouri, Kansas and Oklahoma. Coffeyville is located about sixty miles west of Joplin in Ozark foothills that sprawl into Kansas, just north of the Oklahoma border. Coffeyville was a peaceful little town back in 1892, a hub of the Union Pacific Railroad where not even the marshal carried a gun. The Daltons lived in Coffeyville and were familiar with the layout of the town, and even though it was incredibly ill-advised to rob the banks in your own town—where everybody knows you—they likely would have gotten away with the robberies that October morning but for a few things that were out of order.

Coffeyville was in the process of paving some of its downtown streets, and the very hitching posts to which the gang had planned to tether their horses had been removed. Instead, the outlaws tied their mounts to a fence in a narrow passage known today as Death Alley. Walking from the alley

150

with Bob Dalton as the leader, they crossed an open plaza to enter the two unsuspecting banks. But they were vulnerable in the open, and they'd been identified by townspeople, who ran to a hardware store to obtain Winchesters and ammunition in order to defend the banks.

Backing the Daltons were two experienced charter members of the gang: Dick Broadwell and Bill Powers. Broadwell, son of a good Kansas family, went to the wrong side of the law when a young lady stole his heart and his bankroll and left him flat in Fort Worth. Powers was a Texas boy who had punched cows down on the Cimarron.

On the day of the robberies, Grat Dalton grouped with Powers and Broadwell and led them into the Condon Bank. Emmett and Bob paired up and went on to the First National. Once inside, they began collecting money as Coffeyville citizens were already preparing to take them on.

After more than 120 years, gruesome details linger of the citizens' attack on the robbers. Four citizens and four outlaws (Grat and Bob Dalton, Dick Broadwell and Bill Powers) were killed. Emmett Dalton was seriously wounded but survived twenty-three gunshot wounds.

While most historians agree that there were five raiders, some claim that there was a sixth rider who fled. Several theories exist as to who the sixth rider was, but most likely it was Bill Dalton, the gang's scout and informant. In a postmortem photograph, Bill Powers, Bob Dalton, Grat Dalton and Dick Broadwell appear handcuffed and placed side by side displayed on a platform in Death Alley. As told to me during an interview with Mr. Brent Craven of Coffeyville's Dalton Museum, the Winchester lying on Bob and Grat Dalton belonged to Grat and is now a historical artifact that belongs to the museum.

When asked, Mr. Craven went on to explain why all four of the robbers are in their stocking feet, without shoes. He said that the townspeople had taken the shoes as souvenirs, along with fragments of the fabric of their clothing they had torn off. In order to protect the corpses, the town sheriff put the bodies in jail cells.

Emmett was the baby of the lot, only age twenty-one on the day of the raid but already an experienced robber. At Coffeyville, Emmett had money from the First National bank mounted on his horse and had started to ride out of town, but seeing Bob shot down, he returned and attempted to help him onto his horse. Emmett was badly wounded and placed under guard at Dr. Wells's office, where his wounds were dressed. He had been shot through the right arm below the shoulder (the bone was crushed) and through the left hip and groin; he also had about twenty pieces of buckshot in the back.

MISSOURI OZARKS LEGENDS & LORE

In agony, he fought for his life when eight others had already died, but he wasn't expected to survive. At eleven o'clock, Emmett Dalton was still alive but suffering in agony and not expected to survive another day. William Dalton arrived from Oklahoma and attended to his brother, as if the bandit were an innocent young boy. Emmett's condition continued to decline, and it seemed that there was no hope he'd recover.

Two days later, witnesses were allowed to be present when Emmett was examined by Dr. Wells. They described a young man lying on a bed, with an attractive face, clear eyes, a good complexion, regular features and a smooth voice.

Bodies were carried in for Emmett to identify. First up was a tall, raw-boned man with prominent features whom Emmett identified through tear-filled eyes and with a quivering voice as Bob Dalton, the favored brother he idolized to the point of hero worship. Next, he broke down again as Graton was brought in—the brother who had always been looking for a fight. He also identified the other bandits, stating details that had been planned for the robbery, including Bob claiming that he could one-up the James Gang's record by robbing two banks in one day. When Emmett told them he didn't want any part of it, they said he'd better go along and help in order to have money to leave the country. They said if he stayed around here, he'd get caught or killed. They were going anyway, so for the love of his brothers, Emmett joined the raid knowing that he'd be accused either way—and he had no money to leave the country anyway.

The *New York Times* of October 8, 1892, reported that Ben Dalton had been sick in bed at home on the farm, four miles north of Kingfisher, when he received the news of this awful affair. He managed to come with Adeline and other family but distanced himself from the outlaws, underscoring that he was a farmer and a good citizen with no ill will to the people of Coffeyville. The *Dallas Morning News* of October 10, 1892, noted that Emmett Dalton's condition was so greatly improved that it was considered probable that he'd recover. After Emmett's stay in jail at Independence, friends named Star and Kansan summed him up as having made friends with everyone he met, and a gentleman not given to boasting. They attributed a thousand pities that a young man so endowed by nature with charm that would deliver him success in any honorable calling should drift into a life that made him a menace to the peace and order of society.

Emmett miraculously survived the wounds he received in Coffeyville. He was tried and convicted and sentenced to life in prison, where he was a model prisoner who gained a full pardon after only fourteen years. While in prison,

152

his mother, Adeline Lee Younger Dalton, visited him twice yearly between 1892 and 1908, making the three-hundred-mile round-trip consistently as she aged from fifty-seven to seventy-one.

According to Mr. Brent Craven of the Dalton Museum, Coffeyville was a hub of the Union Pacific Railroad and had a direct line to Lansing, Kansas, where Emmett was serving his sentence. It's only logical that Adeline Dalton traveled by train to visit Emmett and petition for clemency. In Brent Craven's explanation, the warden granted full pardon based on Adeline's persistence (also Emmett was an expensive prisoner with a frail medical condition and need for surgeries).

Concluding my conversation with Brent Craven, I thanked him for taking the time to talk to me. "I should let you go. You sound busy, and I don't want to hold you up any longer."

To that he replied, "With your connection to the Daltons, you should be careful about using those words around here." Where would we be in this upside-down world without spontaneous humor?

Emmett returned to Kingfisher, lived with Adeline and finished the manuscript for his first book, *Beyond the Law 1908*. Mr. Craven noted during our interview that Emmett returned to Coffeyville after his pardon and was well received by the townspeople.

After his 1908 release, Emmett married his childhood sweetheart, the twice-widowed Julia Johnson Gilstrap Lewis, in September 1908 in Oklahoma. Emmett claimed that she had faithfully waited for him to be released from prison; however, the facts prove that notion to be far-fetched.

Emmett claimed in *When the Daltons Rode* that he was motivated to write the book in order to set the record straight on the Dalton Gang. Due to the sensationalism that surrounded the Dalton Gang's exploits, they were accused of robberies all over the country but had operated chiefly in Kansas and Oklahoma Territory. Skeptics claim that Emmett left out a lot of their exploits and elevated the reputation of Bob Dalton by design.

In 1908, Emmett published *Beyond the Law*. He and Julia moved to Hollywood, where Emmett acted in the movie of the same title. This and other films based on his life toured the theaters as secondary features. In 1925, Emmett toured and lectured with *Beyond the Law* until early 1925. He became a general manager in two film companies, Southern Feature Film Corporation and Standard Pictures of California Inc. Adeline Dalton died that same year. In January 1931, Emmett published *When the Daltons Rode*, written in collaboration with Jack Jungmeyer. In April–May, Emmett and Julia took a long automobile tour from California through Oklahoma and

Kansas. In Coffeyville, Emmett commissioned a marker for the grave of Bob, Grat and Bill Powers.

After being diagnosed with diabetes mellitus in 1932, Emmett retired from the real estate business, and his health deteriorated. He spent time writing movie scenarios and stories for western magazines. On July 4, 1937, Emmett suffered a stroke, and he died on July 13, 1937, at home in Hollywood, California. He was cremated and buried in Kingfisher, Oklahoma.

The Impartial Friend: Death, the only immortal who treats us all alike, whose pity and whose peace and whose refuge are for all—the soiled and the pure, the rich and the poor, the loved and the unloved.
—*Mark Twain*, last written statement,
in *Paine's Moments with Mark Twain*

BIBLIOGRAPHY

Ashley, Mike, ed. *The Giant Book of Myths and Legends*. N.p.: MetroBooks, an imprint of Friedman/Fairfax Publishers, 1996.

Bretz, Harlen. *Caves of Missouri*. Missouri Geological Survey and Water Resources, 1956.

Cheung, Theresa. *The Element Encyclopedia of the Psychic World, A-Z: The Ultimate of Spirits, Mysteries, and the Paranormal*. New York: HarperCollins Publishers Ltd., 2006.

Dallas Morning News. October 10, 1892.

Dalton, Emmett. *Beyond the Law*. 1st ed. Gretna, LA: Pelican Publishing, 1918.

Devereaux, Paul. *Spirit Roads: An Exploration of Otherworldly Routes*. London: Collins and Brown, an imprint of Anova Books Company Ltd., 2007.

DuBose, Fred, ed. "See the USA the Easy Way: 136 Loop Tours to 1200 Great Places." *Reader's Digest*, 1995.

From the Prison Ledger. "Emmett Dalton." Kansas State Historical Society.

Genī. "Colonel Charles Lee Younger (Will and Testament)." https://www.geni.com.

Journal of the Missouri Speleological Survey 58. "History of the Lemp Brewery Caverns & Cherokee Cave" (2018).

Kindred Moon Paranormal Lemp Mansion. Documentary, 2014. Available on Amazon Prime.

Mezrich, Ben. *The 37th Parallel: The Secret Truth Behind America's UFO Highway*. New York: Simon & Schuster, 2016.

Bibliography

Missouri Speleology 6, no. 3. "Cherokee Cave, St. Louis, Missouri?" (1964).

Missouri Speleology 6, no. 4. "Bats/Cherokee Cave" (October 1964).

Momo: The Missouri Monster. Directed by Seth Breedlove. Small Town Monsters LLC documentary, 2019.

My Kindred. "Emmett Dalton's List of the Children of James and Adeline Dalton—Bea Elizabeth 'Dalton' Hoax." https://mykindred.com/dalton/hoax/EmmettsList.php.

Official Manual of the State of Missouri. Jefferson City, MO: Secretary of State, 1979–80, 1,486.

Randolph, Vance. *Ozark Magic and Folklore*. Toronto, CAN: Columbia University Press, 1947.

Randolph, Vance, and George P. Wilson. *Down in the Holler: A Gallery of Ozark Folk Speech*. Norman: University of Oklahoma Press, 1953.

Ronnberg, Ami, editor in chief. *The Book of Symbols: Reflections on Archetypical Images*. Cologne, DE: Taschen, 2010.

Rossiter, Phyllis. *Rural Missouri* 42, no. 3 (March 1989): 16.

Rother, Hubert, and Charlotte Rother. *The Lost Caves of St. Louis*. N.p.: Virginia Publishing, 1996.

Tremeear, Janice. *Haunted Ozarks*. Charleston, SC: The History Press, 2018.

Twain, Mark. "The Great Earthquake in San Francisco." *New York Weekly Review*, November 25, 1865.

Internet Resources

http://anomalyinfo.com/Stories/mark-twains-prophetic-dream.

http://hauntedplaces.org.

http://www.lempmansion.com.

http://www.missourighosts.net/emmaushomesstories.html.

http://www.theozarktraveler.com/sw-missouri/ghosts-and-haunted-places.

http://www.twainquotes.com/Water.html.

http://www.ufonut.com.

https://en.wikipedia.org/wiki/Arcadia,_Missouri.

https://en.wikipedia.org/wiki/Dalton_Gang.

https://en.wikipedia.org/wiki/Gus%27_Pretzels.

https://en.wikipedia.org/wiki/Ste._Genevieve_Historic_District.

https://glorecords.blm.gov/details/patent/default.aspx?accession=OK0460_318&docClass=STA&sid=xxmojfny.bcp#patentDetailsTabIndex=1.

https://katytrailmo.com/katy-trail-maps.

Bibliography

https://law.justia.com/codes/arkansas/2010/title-1/chapter-4/1-4-105.

https://mostateparks.com/park/grand-gulf-state-park.

https://s1.sos.mo.gov/records/archives/archivesdb/birthdeath.

https://traveltips.usatoday.com.

https://vacationidea.com/missouri/best-caves-in-missouri.htm.

https://www.areawidenews.com/story/1582679.

https://www.atlasobscura.com/places/city-museum.

https://www.atlasobscura.com/places/fantastic-caverns.

https://www.atlasobscura.com/places/ozark-spooklight.

https://www.atlasobscura.com/places/ralph-foster-museum-beverly-hillbillies-car.

https://www.atlasobscura.com/places/taum-sauk-mountain.

https://www.atlasobscura.com/places/venice-cafe.

https://www.britannica.com/place/Taum-Sauk-Mountain.

https://www.findagrave.com/memorial/33652681/james-lewis-dalton.

https://www.findagrave.com/memorial/33653567/william-marion-dalton.

https://www.historynet.com/dalton-gang.

https://www.morsemillhotel.com/blog.

https://www.news-leader.com.

https://www.nps.gov/buff/index.htm.

https://www.nps.gov/home/learn/historyculture/abouthomesteadactlaw.htm.

https://www.oldcaledonian.com.

https://www.paranormaltaskforce.com/rosebed.html.

https://www.roadsideamerica.com/story/12188.

https://www.roadsideamerica.com/story/23134.

https://www.slu.edu/news.

https://www.tshaonline.org/handbook/entries/dalton-gang.

https://www.upi.com.

ts.net/emmaushomesstories.html.

www.ufont.com.

ABOUT THE AUTHOR

Cynthia McRoy Carroll is the author of *Arkansas Ozark's Legends and Lore*, published February 2020 by The History Press, and now *Missouri Ozarks Legends and Lore*.

A native of the Cave State, she's a Missouri girl whose ancestors settled Madison County in the early 1800s during the westward expansion. In what seems like a contradiction of enormous consequence, other Missouri ancestors trace to the venerated, yet infamous, Dalton Outlaws, who robbed trains and banks in the American Wild West.

With experience as a former licensed interior designer, instructor and tour coordinator for the Museum of Fine Arts Houston, she presents a unique inroad to the Missouri Ozarks. History, geology and architecture are the heart and soul of this collection, underscored by a mystical vibe.

Her interest in historic architecture and preservation stems from her childhood in the historic St. Louis neighborhoods of Soulard and Benton Park during the Atomic Age. She studied interior design and fine art at Lone Star College and the Glassell School of Art. With an interest in folklore and legend, haunts and everything inexplicable, she attends conferences that feature folklore, myth, UFO phenomena and other mystical topics—just for fun.

She and her husband live in The Woodlands, Texas, in the piney forest near the Gulf of Mexico, where they enjoy time with family and exploring the great state of Texas.

Visit us at
www.historypress.com